THE WAY OF THE GLADIATOR

THE
WAY OF
THE
GLADIATOR

DANIEL P. MANNIX

INTEGRATED MEDIA
NEW YORK

Previously published as *Those About to Die*

Copyright © 1958, 2001 by Daniel P. Mannix
Foreword copyright © 2001 by Michael Stephenson

ISBN: 978-1-5040-9088-9

This edition published in 2024 by Open Road Integrated Media, Inc.
180 Maiden Lane
New York, NY 10038
www.openroadmedia.com

FOREWORD

"... A place without justice or mercy, where only the smart or
ruthless could survive."

I first read Daniel Mannix's mind-boggling history of the Roman
Games when I was about 14. I think I read it at one sitting or,
more probably, huddled under the bedsheets with a flashlight
so no one would see my eyeballs popping out with amazement
at the bloodletting in the Coliseum. Although his gore-dipped
history is based on the evidence and accounts of the period,
Mannix (his very name sounds like a gladiator from conquered
Gaul) had a terrific ability, like a good popular novelist, to make
the scenes come alive, to take you there.

Re-reading it, I can still feel my jaw go slack with astonishment. The staggering numbers involved, the animals and
humans slaughtered, the unspeakable acts of cruelty, are almost
beyond comprehension.

Pompey boasted of having 10,000 men killed over the course
of eight spectacles, and at one show he pitched 20 elephants,
600 lions, and over 400 leopards against Gaetulians armed with
darts; after Trajan's victory over the Dacians, he had 11,000
animals slaughtered by *bestiarii*—gladiators who specialized in

animal-killing. Bulls and jackasses were trained to rape women. Stadia were flooded so that opposing navies could fight to the death; crocodiles and hippos were sent in to the water to attack anyone who had fallen in. In fact, every conceivable way of torturing and killing men, women, and children was devised to amuse, impress, and appease the Roman mob.

The cost, of course, was staggering. One politician complained that "It's cost me three inheritances to stop the mouth of the people." (But, as we all know, it still costs our pols a pretty penny to shove themselves down our throats!)

The gladiators were not all hopeless wretches condemned to certain death. They had their special skills and were proud of them: *reterians* with their trident and net; *secutors* with shield and sword; *dimachaeri* skilled with the dagger; Parthian bowmen; Assyrians and their deadly flails; German javelin specialists; Sikhs from the Indian subcontinent, with their razor-sharp throwing rings; redheaded Irishmen armed only with their skull-splitting *shillelahs;* and the immaculate discipline of the Greek *hoplites.*

They could make money—lots of it if they were particularly skilled and lucky. They could have women—lots of them, and high-born ones, too. And they could win their freedom. In fact, the Roman writer Epictetus says that gladiators used to pray for more fights so they could distinguish themselves and make more money.

One of the great pleasures of this little classic is the way Mannix brings real gladiators to life. Basing his mini-biographies on actual historical evidence, he breathes life and death into characters we only know from grave inscriptions and contemporary historians.

The world of the Roman games so vividly portrayed in *The Way of the Gladiator* seems at first sight to be unbelievable in its ferocity. "That couldn't happen now" we hear ourselves saying. But the Roman populace who screamed with laughter at the sight of fellow humans, defenseless women and children, as well as gladiators, being torn apart by beasts, or roasted alive, or crucified, or hacked to death, cannot be dismissed as safely "ancient." We only need to look into the mouths of the gas chambers, the killing fields of Cambodia, the mass graves of Rwanda and Kosovo to realize that the mob is always with us, and it's always howling for blood.

Michael Stephenson
Former Editor-in-Chief
The Military Book Club

THE WAY OF THE GLADIATOR

I

Nero was emperor and for two-weeks the mob had been rioting uncontrolled in the streets of Rome. The economy of the greatest empire that the world had ever seen was coming apart like an unraveling sweater. The cost of maintaining Rome's gigantic armed forces, equipped with the latest catapults, ballistae, and fast war galleys, was bleeding the nation white and in addition there were the heavy subsidies that had to be paid to the satellite nations dependent on Rome for support. The impoverished government had neither the funds nor the power to stop the riots.

In this crisis, the Captain of the Shipping hurried by chariot to consult with the first tribune.

"The merchant fleet is in Egypt awaiting loading," he announced. "The ships can be loaded either with corn for the starving people or with the special sand used on the track for the chariot races. Which shall it be?"

"Are you mad?" screamed the tribune. "The situation here has got out of control. The emperor's a lunatic, the army's on the edge of mutiny and the people are dying of hunger. For the gods' sake, get the sand! We have to get their minds off their troubles!"

Soon special announcement was made by heralds that the finest chariot races on record would be held at the Circus Maximus. Three hundred pairs of gladiators would fight to the death and twelve hundred condemned criminals would be eaten by lions. Fights between elephants and rhinos, buffalo and tigers, and leopards and wild boars would be staged. As a special feature, twenty beautiful young girls would be raped by jackasses. Admission to the rear seats, free. Small charge for the first thirty-six tiers of seats.

Everything else was promptly forgotten. The gigantic stadium, seating 385,000 people, was jammed to capacity. For two weeks the games went on while the crowd cheered, made bets and got drunk. Once again the government had a breathing space to try to find some way out of its difficulties.

The games—as these incredible spectacles were politely called—were a national institution. Millions of people were dependent on them for a living: animal trappers, gladiator trainers, horse breeders, shippers, contractors, armorers, stadium attendants, promoters and businessmen of all kinds. To have abolished the games would have thrown so many people out of work that the national economy would have collapsed. In addition, the games were the narcotic that kept the Roman mob doped up so the government could operate. A performer named Pylades contemptuously told Augustus Caesar, "Your position depends on how we keep the mob amused." Juvenal wrote bitterly. "The people who have conquered the world now have only two interests—bread and circuses."

In a sense, the people were trapped. Rome had overextended herself. She had become, as much by accident as design, the dominant nation of the world. The cost of maintaining the "Pax Romana"—the Peace of Rome—over most of the known world was proving too great even for the enormous resources of the mighty empire. But Rome did not dare to abandon her allies or pull back her legions who were holding the barbarian tribes in a line extending from the Rhine in Germany to the Persian Gulf. Every time that a frontier post was relinquished, the wild hordes would sweep in, overrun the area and move just that much closer to the nerve centers of Roman trade.

So the Roman government was constantly threatened by bankruptcy and no statesman could find a way out of the difficulty. The cost of its gigantic military program was only one of Rome's headaches. To encourage industry in her various satellite nations, Rome attempted a policy of unrestricted trade, but the Roman workingman was unable to compete with the cheap foreign labor and demanded high tariffs. When the tariffs were passed, the satellite nations were unable to sell their goods to the only nation that had any money. To break the deadlock, the government was finally forced to subsidize the Roman working class to make up the difference between their "real wages" (the actual value of what they were producing) and the wages required to keep up their relatively high standard of living. As a result, thousands of workmen lived on this subsidy and did nothing whatever, sacrificing their standard of living for a life of ease.

The wealthy class of Rome, living in palaces and eating banquets composed of such delicacies as thrushes' tongues in wild honey and sow's udders stuffed with fried baby mice, owed their riches to great factories where slave laborers produced enormous masses of goods by what we now call assembly-line methods. The dispossessed farmers and unemployed workmen had one great cry: "Let the rich pay!" The government responded by increasing taxes year after year on the plutocrats, but there was a point beyond which they dared not go. After all, it was the taxes paid by these rich men that kept the whole system going and the government did not dare to ruin them. Attempts were made to abolish slave labor in the factories but the free workmen's demand for short hours and high wages had grown so great that only slaves could be used economically. Also, the big factory owners were politically powerful and fought every effort to break up their holdings by bribing senators, hiring lobbyists, and securing the support of unscrupulous labor leaders. A Roman factory owner found it far more profitable to spend thousands of sesterces in such practices rather than lose his slaves. And the Roman freeman would far rather have his dole and games than work for a living.

To the Roman mob—caught in an economic tangle it could not comprehend and was unable to break—the circus was the only panacea for its troubles. The great amphitheaters became the ordinary man's temple, home, place of assembly, and ideal. As the games were ostensibly pious ceremonies given in honor of the gods, they gratified his religious sense. He was able for a few hours at least to inhabit an edifice more magnificent than the Golden Palace of Nero instead of a miserable, overcrowded tenement. Here he was able to meet with other freemen, feel a sense of unity as he sat with his faction cheering a certain chariot team, and impose his wishes on the emperor himself for, as the Romans themselves said, "In the circus alone are the people rulers." The Romans worshiped courage and every Roman liked to picture himself as a rough, tough fighter. In Rome, the "little guy" could identify himself with a successful gladiator as a modern fight fan can identify himself with a famous prize fighter.

There were other attractions. Betting ran so high that fortunes were won or lost in the circus within a few minutes, and only by betting could the ordinary freeman obtain wealth. Also, no matter how badly off a Roman might be, he had the satisfaction of knowing that he was superior to the poor wretches in the arena. Although few Romans cared for the low pay and rigid discipline of the army, they could still consider themselves real fighting men as they shouted advice and insults to the struggling gladiators below. Nothing delighted the Roman mob more than to have some visiting dignitary from a satellite nation get sick during the games and have to rush from the amphitheater. The freeman would say with great satisfaction, "Those effeminate Greeks, they can't take the sight of blood like us Romans!" and turn to the next event with renewed relish.

The games—which eventually came to cost one-third of the total income of the empire and used up thousands of animals and humans every month—started out as festivals no more bloodthirsty than the average county fair. The first games in 238 B.C. featured exhibitions of trick riding, acrobats, wire walkers, trained animals, chariot racing and athletic events. There was boxing with soft leather straps over the knuckles that took the place of gloves. The militia staged a sham battle and the crack cavalry Corps, composed of rich young men mounted on thoroughbred horses and dressed in gold and silver armor, went through a drill. There were also horse races in which the riders had to jump from one horse to another in full gallop. Occasionally a pageant was held, such as the Siege of Troy, in which a wooden mockup representing Troy was attacked by militiamen dressed as Greek soldiers and finally burned amid much blowing of trumpets and loud applause. An admission fee was charged by whoever was producing the show.

Later this sort of exhibition got much too tame for the Romans. The only one of the events to last was the chariot racing, which, like modern horse racing, was a perfect sport for betting. However, even the chariot racing completely changed its character. Instead of being simply a race it became bloody and exciting enough to hold popular interest.

The Circus Maximus, the oldest amphitheater in Rome, was especially designed for chariot racing. Although in the early days the games were held in any open field convenient to the city and the chariots simply raced along a course marked off on the ground, I'll describe the Circus Maximus races in about 50 A.D. to give an idea of the sport at its height.

Originally built about 530 B.C., The Circus Maximus measured 1,800 feet long by 600 feet wide—more than twice the size of the Yankee Stadium. It was shaped like a long U. At the open end of the U were the stalls for the chariots, with doors that could all be thrown open at the same instant as in the start of modern horse races. Down the center of the amphitheater ran a long barricade, called the Spine, and the chariots had to circle the Spine seven times—a total distance of about four miles.

The Spine was the show spot of the whole circus. There were statues on columns, fountains spurting perfumed water, altars to the gods, and even a small temple dedicated to the Venus of the Sea, the special patron goddess of charioteers. The chari-oteers always burned incense to this Venus before beginning a race. In the center of the Spine there was an obelisk, imported from Egypt, surmounted by a golden ball. This ball gleamed brilliantly in the sun and was the most noticeable object in the circus. The obelisk, minus the ball, now stands in the center of Saint Peter's Square in Rome, before the cathedral.

Near the ends of the Spine were two columns, each surmounted by a crossbar of marble. On one crossbar was mounted a line of marble eggs. There was a line of dolphins on the other. The eggs were the symbol of Castor and Pollux, the heavenly twins who were the patrons saints of Rome, and the dolphins were sacred to Neptune, the patron of horses. Every time the chariots circled the course, an egg and a dolphin were removed so the crowd could tell how many laps had been run. At the extreme ends of the Spine were set three cones some twenty feet high and ornamented with bas-reliefs. These cones (called metae) acted as bumpers to keep the elegant Spine from being damaged by the chariots on the turns. Pliny says the metae looked like cypress trees.

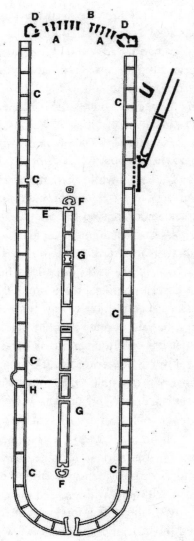

AA. Starting gates
B. Porta Pompae:
    central door for processions.
CC. Lines of seats
DD. Towers of the oppidum

E. Starting gates
FF. Metae.
GG. Spina, set a little diagonally.
H. Tribal Judicum; unpires' seats

The racing was managed by a number of big corporations that were regarded as the most important moneymaking enterprises in the Roman world and had thousands of stockholders. Stock in these companies was so valuable that it was carefully passed on from father to son as a priceless possession. These corporations maintained huge offices in the heart of the business districts in all main cities as well as in Rome itself. In addition to these offices, the companies owned great blocks of buildings near the various circuses (there was a circus of some sort in virtually every town in the empire) and these buildings served as barracks and stables. The buildings were usually set around a track for exercising the teams. The companies also owned countless stud farms and even maintained fleets of ships with built-in stalls for transporting horses from one circus to another. The size of the stud farms may be imagined by the remark of a government agent who, in 550 A.D. when it was finally necessary to abolish the racing, was sent around to break up the farms. He said of one place: "It was already so reduced that the owner has only four hundred horses left so I decided that it was not worth bothering about."

The number of men employed by these companies, including herdsmen, ostlers, drivers, breakers and so on, is unknown, but it is interesting to look at a partial list of the men engaged in the actual race itself. In addition to the charioteers there were the medici (doctors), the aurigatores (the charioteer's assistants), the procuratores dromi (men who smoothed the sand before the race), the conditores (who greased the chariot wheels), the moratores (who grabbed the horses at the end), the sparsores (who cleaned the chariots), the erectores (who took down the eggs and dolphins), and the armentarii (grooms). In addition, there were also the stable-boys, trainers, vets, saddlers, tailors, stable guards, dressers and waterers. There was even a special group who did nothing but talk to the horses and cheer them on as they were being led from their stalls.

The charioteers themselves were mostly slaves, although a few freemen volunteered for the job in hopes of winning fame and fortune. Slave or not, a successful charioteer was the hero of Rome and could win huge sums. Several retired as millionaires, having either bought their freedom or been given it by a grateful master who shared in the winnings. The Emperor Caligula gave Eutychus, a famous charioteer, two million sesterces (about $85,000) as a gift. Crescens, an African who started racing when he was thirteen, won $75,000 before he was killed at twenty-two. He won thirty-eight races "snatched at the post"—that is, came from behind in the last lap to win, which was considered an especially praiseworthy feat. One man won fifteen purses of gold in an hour. Although the usual sum paid to a winning charioteer was only about $2,500, he received much more in bonuses from the company, gifts from admirers, bribes from bettors who wanted tips, and concerns who wanted to use his picture on vases, trays and souvenir cameos.

Probably the most famous charioteer was a little, dark, wiry fellow named Diocles. He was the first man to win a thousand races. Diocles had a passion for horses and fine clothes. He swaggered around Rome in a silk tunic and embroidered linens, and owned his own teams—which was as unusual as for a modern jockey to have a racing stable. Juvenal wrote bitterly: "Decent men groan to see this ex-slave with an income one hundred times that of a senator," but Diocles was a popular idol. He had started life as a slave-groom to a Spanish nobleman, been shipped to Rome with a cargo of horses and bought by a patrician who admired the boy's uncanny skill with temperamental thoroughbreds. He drove his first race at the age of twenty-four and, being a newcomer, was illegally forced to take the outside track. Positions were supposedly chosen by lot but there was a good deal of crookedness about the selections. To reach the rail, an outside chariot had to cut in front of the others, which meant almost certain death. Diocles didn't try it. He tailed the others until the last lap and then by a magnificent piece of driving, passed the other three chariots to win.

It was customary for the owner of a racing stable to split the purse with the charioteer, so Diocles soon made enough money to buy his freedom. He then put his winnings into buying horses, trained them himself, and got his own chariot. He usually drove stallions and collected over $40,000 a year for stud fees alone. In addition to his other privileges, Diocles like all famous charioteers was allowed on certain days to play April Fool-type jokes on anyone he wished, even members of the nobility.

Another lucrative source of income for Diocles was making freak runs for big side bets. Once he raced twice in one day; the first time with a six-horse hitch (swinging a six-in-hand around the ends of the Spine at full speed was a terrific feat) and won 40,000 sesterces. Then he raced a seven-horse hitch not yoked, held only with traces, and won 50,000. Perhaps his most remarkable stunt was winning a race without using a whip, for a side bet of 30,000 sesterces. The whip was used by the charioteers not so much to beat the teams as to guide them on the turns. While rounding the cones at the ends of the Spine at full speed, the charioteer could signal the inside horse when to turn by laying his whip on its shoulder, and if one of the other horses tried to turn too soon, the driver could check him by a light flick. The reins were tied around the charioteer's waist so he could get more leverage on the turns but this made it difficult to control any individual horse.

The horses were extremely valuable, worth far more than slaves. Training started when the horses were three years old and was so detailed that a horse could not be raced until he was five. Some teams were so smart that they could drive themselves. One driver fell out when his team made the usual "jackrabbit" start from the stalls but the horses kept going and actually won the race. They got the prize, too. Sculptors made statues of famous horses, some of which still remain. Under the statues are inscriptions such as: "Tuscus, driven by Fortunatus of the Blues, 386 wins," and "Victor, driven by Guita of the Greens, 429 wins." Lucius Veres had a horse named Volucris who was awarded a bushel of gold pieces after a race, and the Emperor Hadrian put up a mausoleum for his horse, Borysthenes, that still stands. The most famous of these horses was Incitatus, belonging to the Emperor Caligula. Incitatus had a marble bedroom, an ivory manager and drank from a golden bucket. Famous artists decorated the walls of his stall and he attended state dinners where his oats and corn were served to him by his special slaves. Caligula even planned to have him made a consul.

A horse that had won over one hundred races was called a Centenarius and wore a special harness. Diocles owned nine Centenarii, all of which he had trained himself. He had one horse that had won over two hundred races. This horse, named Passerinus, was so revered that soldiers patrolled the streets when he was sleeping to keep people from making any noise. The best horse in the team was always on the near hand (left side) of the hitch and never yoked—only held by traces. On the turns, this horse was nearest to the Spine and his speed and sure-footedness meant the difference between life and death to the driver. The second best horse was on the offside (right) of the hitch and was usually not yoked either. On the turns, he had to jerk the chariot around while the Centenarius on the inside pivoted close to the cones. The two center horses were yoked on either side of the shaft and were mainly for pulling power although the whole team had to know their jobs.

As today, there were unending arguments about the best breeds and best farms. The horses were not shod, so the condition of their feet was crucial. The Sicilian horses were very fast but unreliable, the Iberians good only for a short course (feet too soft), and the Libyan best for a long drag. There were several breeds we do not have today; among them the Orynx, which was striped like a zebra but was apparently a domestic breed of horse.

Although there are innumerable statues of Roman charioteers in museums and although we have plenty of old records of the sport such as "Scorpus of the White Faction got first place seven times, second place twenty-nine times and third place sixty times," I haven't been able to find a detailed description of any single race. However, there are many scattered references to incidents in the races, and it is possible to imagine what a race was like. Let's picture a race during the Ludi Magni (great games) with Diocles one of the drivers.

For weeks, virtually the only topic of conversation in Rome had been the race and the betting odds. People paid huge sums for hot tips, which were usually unreliable. Seneca, the great Roman philosopher, exclaimed: "The art of conversation is dead. Can no one today talk of anything except the skill of various charioteers and the quality of their teams?" Diocles was such a heavy favorite that a senator remarked, "If Diocles loses, it will do more to upset the national economy than a major military defeat." But a few days before the race, the betting odds suddenly altered. All sorts of rumors were sweeping the city. A man had it on the authority of one of the conditores who kept the chariots greased that Diocles had been heavily bribed to throw the race. A tavern keeper had overheard two members of the Praetorian guard say that the emperor, who was backing another team, had arranged with the sponsor of the games to start the race again if Diocles was ahead. The madam of a brothel had it from one of her girls who had entertained the valet of a prominent politician that two of the opposing charioteers had sworn a sacred oath to get Diocles by catching his chariot between them and wrecking it. A man who had a cousin who knew a vet had been told that Diocles' Centenarius, Passerinus, had been doped. People hurried to the stable to taste Passerinus dung to see if the story was true. So the odds went up and down according to the latest rumor, many of them deliberately spread by heavy bettors who were speculating on the event.

The four corporations who controlled the races were known as the White, Red, Green, and Blue, and the charioteers wore tunics of their corporation's color like a jockey's racing silks. All Rome was divided into these four factions—in fact, our word *faction* originally meant a group supporting a chariot team. People wore colored flowers, ribbons or scarfs to show which team they were backing. So devoted were the people to their faction that they often had it engraved on their tombstones: "Memmius Regulus was a good man, a devoted husband and a staunch supporter of the Reds." Nero, who always backed the Greens, had the arena sand dyed green to honor them and the Emperor Vitellius had fifty people killed because they booed the Blues.

On the day of the race, the city was almost deserted, nearly everyone being at the Circus Maximus. Troops had to patrol the empty streets to prevent looting by thieves. The races began at dawn and lasted until sunset. First there was a procession around the arena, led by the editor (the man giving the games), who was usually a politician running for office and needed votes. The editor rode in a chariot dressed in a purple toga as though he were a member of the nobility. Only as an editor of games could an ordinary man wear the purple. Around the chariot walked the editor's ward-heelers in white robes carrying palm branches and after him rode a group of young aristocrats to show that men of wealth and breeding were also supporting the editor. Then came a long procession of priests carrying images of the gods on litters, swinging incense burners and chanting hymns. The crowd had been given handkerchiefs or placards with the editor's political slogan stamped on them ("Vote for Eprius Marcellus, the people's friend") and claques had been organized under cheer leaders to shout a slogan together. As the editor made the rounds, bowing and smiling, the claques all gave their cheers and the rest of the crowd stood up and waved the handkerchiefs or placards and shouted.

When the procession was over, the crowd sat down to study their racing forms and make last-minute bets with the bookies who ran up and down the aisles. Some of the forms, engraved on ivory or brass for the use of the nobility, are still in existence. They look like this:

1st Race

Racing Stable	Team	Color of Horse	Charioteer	Stall
Green	Passerinus	Gray	Diocles	III
	Pomperanus	Gray		
	Tigris	Chestnut		
	Raptore	Black		

And so on for all four teams in the first race.

Although the stalls from which the chariots started were all equidistant from a point midway between the stands and the end of the Spine, the charioteer who had the left-hand stall had an advantage, being able to go straight to the Spine and thus gaining the inside track. The stalls were numbered from one to four and charioteers picked their number out of a bowl. Diocles drew the third stall from the left.

Slaves were out watering the track to keep down dust, raking the sand and making sure no one had thrown any empty wine skins or gnawed bones on the track. A trumpet was blown and the track was hurriedly cleared. Meanwhile in the paddock behind the stalls the charioteers were getting their teams ready. The men wore short tunics that left their arms bare, heavy leather caps like crash-helmets, and each carried a knife in his belt so that in case of an accident he could cut himself free of the reins tied around his waist. Most of the drivers had coated themselves with boar's dung in the belief that the odor kept horses from stepping on a man if he was thrown from his chariot.

The racing chariots were very light, made of wood with bronze fittings. They were lower and had a wider wheel base than the ordinary chariot. When the trumpet sounded to clear the track, teams were led out by their handlers and hitched up. There were several types of hitch used. Although the most usual was to have the two center horses on either side of the shaft yoked together and the two outside horses on traces, sometimes a driver would have only his left-hand horse on traces. On rare occasions the entire team might be on traces to give them greater maneuverability. The horses' tails were always tied up so they wouldn't foul the reins.

The hitching-up must have been quite a sight—the horses pawing the ground and snorting, their manes studded with pearls and semi-precious stones. They wore breastplates hung with gold and silver amulets and each horse had a broad ribbon the color of his racing stable around his neck. The Romans claimed that chariot racing improved the breed of horses but actually these animals were so inbred and temperamental that they were unfitted for anything except this breakneck dash around the arena at top speed.

Another trumpet sounded, the drivers took their places in the gleaming chariots and the grooms led the teams into the stalls, entering them from the rear. Then the grooms got out of the way—fast. A moment's pause. The editor of the games rose in his box and dropped a handkerchief. The gates of the four stalls were thrown open at the same instant and the chariots were off.

Every driver tried to reach the inside track around the Spine. As a result, there were usually so many crack-ups in this first wild rush that a special gate had to be constructed under the stands near the starting point where the arena attendants could drag out the smashed chariots, dead men and horses so they wouldn't block the course when the rest had circled the Spine and started the second lap. Sometimes the race never got going at all—all the chariots ending up in a pile at this point.

To solve this problem, a white rope called the Alba Linea was stretched from the Spine to the stands, just high enough to trip a galloping team of horses. A judge who was stationed in a box could drop this rope if he decided that it was a fair start. If the chariots didn't get away together or if there was too much jostling and fouling, at the start, he left the rope up and then the race had to start over again.

This rope posed a very critical decision for the charioteers. If a driver went all out to reach the preferred inside track around the Spine and the rope wasn't dropped in time, he and his chariot went wheels over shaft. If he held back too much and the rope was dropped at the last instant, some other driver got ahead of him. It helped to know the judge's prejudices. If he was a secret supporter of the Blues and the Blue chariot was left at the post, he'd keep the rope up. If Blue was ahead, he'd drop the rope no matter what.

In this race, we'll suppose that all the chariots got away to an even start and the rope was dropped as the foremost chariot approached it. We can be pretty sure that this foremost chariot wasn't Diocles. He was famous for holding his team back until the last lap and then coming from behind to win. Diocles might even have been running last as the four chariots swept around the cones at the far end of the Spine on their first turn.

The basic strategy of all charioteering was to take the turns as tight as possible, but there were many other tricks. If ahead, you tried to block the others so they couldn't pass. If you were in the middle, you cut in front of the other chariots on the turns to force the drivers to rein in. If you got the chance, you hooked your wheel inside the wheel of an opposing chariot and then suddenly swung your team out. If properly done, it could jerk your opponent's wheel off the axle and put him out of the race.

We'll suppose that by the end of the fifth lap, Orestes, a Greek driving for the Reds, is ahead of Diocles, driving for the Greens, just behind. Diocles is using his whip only on three of the horses, controlling Passerinus, his inside horse, by voice alone. Orestes is a skillful driver and as they go into the sixth lap, he manages to block Diocles on the turns so the Spaniard can't pass him. Then the two chariots level out for the rush down the lefthand side of the Spine. In spite of everything Orestes can do, Diocles pulls up alongside of him—but on the outside. They still have one more turn around the end of the Spine, and Orestes cuts it as close as he dares—Diocles turning with him.

As they spin around, Orestes slackens his reins too much while his team is making the swing. His axlerod hits one of the cones and breaks. Orestes is thrown out and as he falls, he tries to jerk out the knife in his belt to cut himself free of the reins. He can't get it free in time. Diocles has had to throw all his weight back on his reins to keep from being entangled in the wreck ahead for the pull of the dragging axle-bar has swung Orestes' team in front of him. Orestes is dragged along by his frantic horses; one moment he's half standing and then he's feet uppermost. The other two chariots following the leaders see their chance and try to pass, but Diocles shouts to his team and gives them their heads. They plow through the wreckage of, Orestes's chariot, trampling the Greek underfoot. Passerinus trips and almost falls but Diocles grabs the stallion's reins in both hands and keep his head up. Now they're through the wreckage and in the clear. One final burst of speed and they cross the finish line while the crowd goes wild, Orestes' corpse is so trampled that, as a contemporary writer remarked after the race, "His best friend couldn't have identified the body."

Diocles retired at forty-two with a fortune of 35 million sesterces (about $1,800,000). We know so much about him because he published a book of memoirs, ghost-written by a contemporary sports writer. Diocles claims to have been the greatest charioteer of all time (he was undoubtedly the most successful financially) although he admits some other drivers won more races than he did. "But what kind of races?" he asks. "On some provincial track running against a lot of plugs. Now, I was always in the big-time events at the Circus Maximus, running against stiff competition. No other driver ever won over a thousand races under those conditions."

Very few charioteers were as lucky at Diocles. Fuscus was killed at twenty-four after only fifty-seven wins. Aurelius Mollicus, judging from his double name a freeman, not a slave, was killed at twenty after a hundred and twenty-five wins. However, all these men had statues made in their honor with glowing inscriptions which were intended to, and have, made them immortal. The inscriptions read: "Never lost the lead at the Ludi Plebei!" "Came from behind to win at the Ludi

Apollinares." "An unknown who really fooled the wise ones."
And so on. There they stand in museums for the benefit of tour-
ists, good-looking men most of them, with powerful forearms
and tremendous shoulders. They lived high, wide and handsome and their end generally came under the flashing hoofs
of horses while the crowd yelled with excitement or thought:
"There go my ten sesterces."

It was often said: "The great spectacle at the circus is not the
games but the spectators." The games were the great emotional
outlet for the mob and they made the most of it. During a race
the crowd literally went mad. Women collapsed or had sexual
orgasms. Men bit themselves, tore their clothes, did mad dances,
bet until they ran out of money and then bet themselves to a
slave dealer to raise more. One man fainted when the White
team fell behind. When the Whites came forward to win in the
last lap, the man had to be revived to be told of his good luck.
Travelers approaching Rome could hear the roar of triumph
when the race was over before they could see the city towers. If
a faction thought that its team had got a raw deal, they staged
a riot—on one occasion setting fire to the Circus Maximus
and burning it to the ground. It was after that a law was passed
saying that all amphitheaters had to be built of stone, although
the upper tiers were still frequently made of wood.

This mania even had a name—it was called Hippomania:
horse-madness. When Felix, a famous charioteer for the Reds,
was killed in a race and his body burned on a funeral pyre, a man
threw himself into the flame so he could perish with his idol. A
nobleman's little boy, when asked what of all things on earth he
wished as a gift, asked for the tunic worn by a famous charioteer
for the Greens. When the Germans were attacking Carthage, the
people refused to defend the walls—they were busy watching a
chariot race. When Treves was burned by the barbarian hordes,

the city council pointed out that the disaster had its good side. "Now we'll have room to build a really fine chariot course in the middle of the city," the governor pointed out.

To show how the passion for chariot racing grew: In 169 B.C. there was one race a day during the games, held late in the afternoon as a climax to the sport. Under Augustus Caesar at the time of Christ, there were twelve races a day. Under Caligula forty years later, there were twenty-four races a day. Two more racing corporations were formed so that six chariots competed instead of the usual four. Later, the number was increased to twelve and even sixteen chariots, but by then the mob had lost all interest in real driving and only wanted to see a lot of smash-ups.

II

In the early days when the games were merely athletic contests there were no gladiatorial combats. Gladiators were introduced by accident. Two brothers named Marcus and Decimus Brutus wanted to give their dead father a really bang-up funeral. The brothers were wealthy patricians, the ruling class in Rome, and providing outstanding funeral rites for a dead parent was an important social obligation. The usual processions, sacrificial animals and prayers weren't enough for the brothers, but Marcus came up with an idea.

"There was an old custom, dating back to prehistoric times, of having a few slaves fight to the death over the grave of some great leader," he reminded his brother. "Why not revive it to show how much we revere the memory of the old man?"

Decimus turned the suggestion over in his mind. Originally this ceremony had been a sort of human sacrifice and the souls of the dead slaves were supposed to serve the chieftain in the next world. The fighting was to make sure that only brave men capable of being good followers would follow the dead leader. Educated Romans like the Brutus brothers didn't believe this old superstition but the dead man had been a great soldier and fond of rough sports.

"Nothing would please father more," he admitted. "If the priests agree, we'll do it. Our social position will be definitely established."

The priests had no objections and half of Rome turned out to watch the fight. Three pairs of slaves fought and the crowd loved it. The brothers became the most popular men in Rome for having put on such a good show. Politicians, eager to be elected, decided to put on similar exhibitions. The following statistics will show how fast the idea caught on:

264 B.C.—	3 pairs of slaves.
216 B.C.—	22 pairs of slaves.
183 B.C.—	60 pairs of slaves.
145 B.C.—	90 pairs fought for three days.

Soon it was taken for granted that anyone running for office had to put on slave fights—the bigger the better.

Promoters began to buy up able-bodied slaves, criminals and prisoners of war especially for these fights. The promoters would then rent the men out at so much per head to any ambitious politician. These professional slave-fighters became known as "gladiators," meaning "swordsmen."

As long as only a few gladiators were engaged, the fights were generally given in the Forum, but when several dozen fought there wasn't enough room. So the fights were moved to the Circus and the gladiators staged their combats as an extra attraction together with the chariot races, the acrobats, the wild animal trainers and the other performers. Unless the show was subsidized by some wealthy man in honor of his ancestors, an admission fee was charged and the whole affair was strictly a business proposition, but later politicians started putting on the shows for free to get votes, or the government staged them to keep the mob quiet.

Unfortunately, no gladiator was kind enough to leave a collection of memoirs or, if any did, the manuscript hasn't survived. However, we know plenty about them as many of the Roman writers such as Suetonius, Martial and Tacitus describe the fights in considerable detail. We know, for example, that one of the most famous gladiators was named Flamma and, although we know very little else about him except a list of his outstanding triumphs, we can by combining stories about several of the gladiators give a reasonably accurate picture of one of these professional killers.

Let's suppose that Flamma was a huge, heavy-set bull of a man. Most gladiators were, as their statues and the portraits of them cut on monuments show. He may well have been a private soldier, condemned to the arena for insubordination. We know of one such case and we'll suppose the man involved was Flamma.

Flamma, then, had been given a bawling-out by a young officer, fresh out of military school and he told the officer off. The officer struck him with a cane and Flamma knocked him down. For this offense, he was sentenced to the arena.

Flamma hoped to be matched against some other ex-soldier and fight with regulation sword and shield, which he knew how to handle, but the penalty for striking an officer was death and the high brass was determined that Flamma wouldn't leave the arena alive. So he was put into one of the new "novelty acts" which were springing up. The Roman mob had tired of the standard combats so the promoters invented fights between a Retiarius, who wore no armor but carried a net and a trident (a three-pronged spear), and a Secutor, who was equipped as a Gaul; that is, he had a fish insignia on his helmet as did the Gauls, and carried a sword and shield. He wore a breastplate and his right arm and left leg were protected by armor. His left arm and right leg were bare to give him greater freedom of movement. Except for its fish symbol, the helmet was very plain so as not to offer a spot where the Retiarius' net or trident could catch. Flamma was to play the part of the Secutor or "chaser." It was up to him to catch the nimble Retiarius or "netman."

The edges of the Retiarius' net were fringed with small lead weights, so when the net was thrown it would open to form a circle. Similar nets are still used by fishermen in various parts of the world today. If he could succeed in catching the Secutor in his net, the Retiarius could pull the heavily armed man off balance and dispatch him with the trident. The Retiarius always had the advantage in these fights and, even with well-trained gladiators, the betting was generally five to three on the netman. In this case, Flamma knew nothing about the business, while the Retiarius was an expert. The odds on the Retiarius were fifty to one with no takers.

When Flamma appeared in the arena in his Gaul's outfit, he was greeted by boos and catcalls from the mob. They knew he was a mutineer and also he was nothing but a palooka who couldn't be expected to put up an interesting fight. Flamma was a fairly simple fellow and his spirit had been broken by the court-martial and the sentence. When he saw that everyone was against him, he dropped his sword and sat down to let the Retiarius finish him off. The crowd, feeling that they had been swindled, burst into shouts of "Chicken!" "What's he afraid of?" "Why does he die so sulkily?" "Whip him!" "Burn him!"—for a gladiator who refused to fight was whipped and prodded with hot irons until he changed his mind. But Flamma's whole regiment had turned out for the fight and they stood up in the stands, shouting for him. When Flamma heard their familiar voices, he picked up his sword and cried, "All right, boys, I'll do my best for the honor of the regiment!" The Retiarius had been parading the arena, taking bows and making dates with the pretty girls for after the fight. Now he settled his net and came for the soldier.

As he approached Flamma, the Retiarius sang the traditional chant of his profession: "I seek not you, I seek a fish. Why do you flee from me, O Gaul?" meanwhile making tentative casts with his net. Then he pretended to slip and fall, hoping to get Flamma off balance. When that didn't work, he danced around the heavily armored man, calling him a coward and daring him to come on, but Flamma had too much sense to wear himself out chasing the agile Retiarius around the arena. He stood his ground and made the other man come to him.

The Retiarius circled him, holding the net by one end and slinging it at Flamma's feet, hoping to have the long net wrap around the Secutor's legs and trip him. Then he suddenly changed his technique and threw the net in a cast. Flamma turned it with his shield but one of the lead pellets hit him in the left eye, partially blinding him. The Retiarius saw his chance and, rushing in, knocked the sword out of the soldier's hand with his trident. Both men ran for the sword but the light Retiarius got there first and threw the sword into the stands. Then he turned to finish off the unarmed man.

It seemed as though Flamma was through but the Retiarius made the mistake of first showing off with some fancy net casts. Flamma managed to give the trident a kick that sent it flying across the arena. The terrified Retiarius turned to run after it, but before he could get away, Flamma grabbed him by the tunic. As the Retiarius went down on his knees, Flamma gave him a rabbit punch with the edge of the shield and killed him.

The victory, although totally unexpected, didn't seem to help Flamma. The emperor simply signaled for another Retiarius to come out and finish him off. But here the condemned man got a break. Flamma's nickname around the barracks was "loach," as loaches have whiskers like a catfish and Flamma had a bristling beard. The soldiers in the stands had been yelling: "Go it, loach!" and the crowd had taken up the yell after Flamma showed that he was really willing to fight. Now a "loach" had killed a "fisherman" and the crowd thought this was such a joke that they demanded that Flamma be spared. Very few emperors dared to ignore the will of the people in the circus. Often notorious bandits and murderers were saved in this way, to the indignation of the judges. So Flamma was sent to gladiatorial school to learn his new trade.

There were four big gladiatorial schools in Italy at this time (about 10 A.D. under Augustus Caesar). They were known as The Great School, The Gallic, The Dacian and the School for Bestiarii (animal fighters). Later, there were dozens of schools maintained by rich enthusiasts of the fights just as today rich men have racing stables. Flamma was sent to The Great School in Rome. No vestige of this school remains but the gladiatorial school in Pompeii is still in good condition, so I'll describe that, although The Great School must have been much bigger.

The school was a rectangular building some 170 feet by 140 feet with an open court in the middle where the men could practice. Around the court ran a roofed passage with small rooms opening into it rather like a cloister. The rooms were only ten by twelve feet, but each man had his cell where he could be alone. There was a kitchen, a hospital, an armory, quarters for the trainers and the guards, and even a graveyard. There was also a prison with leg irons, shackles, branding irons and whips. Opening into the prison was a room used for solitary confinement with a ceiling so low a man couldn't sit up and so short he couldn't stretch out his legs. The remains of four gladiators were found in the Pompeian prison—the men had been unable to escape when the city was covered with the lava flow from Mount Vesuvius. The school was owned by a big promoter but was actually run by an old ex-gladiator who knew all the tricks. These trainers were called lanistae.

Every precaution was taken to keep the gladiators well guarded. The Romans never forgot the lesson they had learned in 72 B.C. when a gladiator named Spartacus with seventy of his comrades escaped from the school and took refuge in the crater of Mount Vesuvius. As all these men were professional fighters, getting them out of the crater was quite a problem. They were joined by escaped slaves, robber bands and discontented peasants. Under Spartacus' leadership, this band of outlaws defeated two Roman generals and seized all southern Italy. They nearly captured Rome itself before being wiped out by legions hastily recalled from the frontiers.

Flamma first had to take an oath: "To suffer myself to be whipped with rods, burned with fire or killed with steel if I disobey." Then he was given a cell whose previous occupant had been killed in the last games.

There was a stone shelf that served as a bed, with a straw-filled mattress on it, and a niche in the wall where Flamma could keep a statue of whatever god he fancied. There was no other furniture. On the walls were scratched girls' names with addresses below them, pictures of naked women, "Sabinus hie" (Kilroy was here), prayers to various gods, dirty cracks about the gladiator master and the dates of fights. In Pompeii, these drawings still survive. There were also a few crude drawings of actual combats—a Secutor enveloped in the net but still stabbing at the Retiarius with his sword, and some fights between different types of gladiators. Over one figure was scribbled "Bebrix, 20 wins" and over another "Nobilior, 11 wins." Nobilior was down, making the sign for mercy to the crowd by holding up one finger of his left hand. Below him was the sign Θ which meant "killed."

Being a phlegmatic man and used to iron discipline, Flamma settled down in the school without much difficulty. Other gladiators had more trouble. The barracks had to be constantly patrolled night and day to make sure the men didn't commit suicide, but even so some men were able to outwit the guards. One man, on his way to the school in a cart, managed to stick his head in the turning wheel and broke his neck. Another man took a pottery bowl in which he was given water, broke it into small pieces, and then ate the pieces. Flamma couldn't understand what was bothering these men. The food was fine, the bed comfortable, and girls were brought in once a week. He had to fight only about twenty times a year and there were no long marches, sudden ambushes or long campaigns as in the army. Frankly, he'd never had it so good.

For the first few weeks Flamma practiced sword strokes against a wooden pole in the exercise court and then against a dummy hung from a pole under the direction of the lanista. He had to learn to use his left hand as readily as his right, as some fighters were suckers for a good southpaw. In order to build up his muscle, the weapons given him were twice as heavy as the ones he'd use in the arena. Then he fought other gladiators using blunt weapons. At last real bouts were put on, but stopped when one man was wounded.

The men all messed at a long table and their meals were carefully prepared by expert dietitians. They were fed a great deal of meat and barley—meat because of its protein content and barley because, so it was believed, the rich grain covered the arteries with a layer of fat and so helped to prevent a man from bleeding to death from a wound.

Perhaps what sold Flamma on being a gladiator more than

anything else was the beautiful armor he was allowed to wear in the arena. As the son of poor Italian peasants, he had never owned anything really impressive in his life and was a pretty simple fellow anyhow. (Right up to the first World War, soldiers insisted on wearing full dress into battle and many a man frankly joined the army so he could wear a busby or a nice red uniform with brass buttons. Even today a general has seriously claimed that the reason so many men join the Marines is that the Marine Corps still retains its ornate full dress, and maybe the general is right.) To a man like Flamma, fine armor meant a lot. His helmets had ostrich or peacock feathers. His breastplates were inlaid with gold and silver. His sword hilt was set with precious stones. His bronze shield was covered with brass studs and painted a brilliant red on the inside. Designs showing gladiatorial fights were engraved on his brassards and cuisses by famous artists. Slaves kept everything polished up for him so that all Flamma had to do was wear the stuff—very different from the army where he'd had to shine his equipment himself.

The trainer watched Flamma's style carefully and decided to use him as a Postulati, fighting in full armor with a sword and lead mace against all comers, who were allowed to use any weapon that they wished.

Flamma's first public appearance as a professional gladiator was at ludi privati (privately sponsored games) given by a politician. For weeks before the event, professional sign writers had toured the city writing ads for the games everywhere they could find space—even on tombstones. There are still old tombstones in Roman burying grounds with the inscription: "Post no bills" engraved on them. Here's a typical ad written on a wall with red paint:

"Weather permitting, 30 pairs of gladiators, furnished by A. Clodius Flaccus, together with substitutes in case any get killed too quickly, will fight May 1st, 2nd and 3rd at the Circus Maximus. The fights will be followed by a big wild beast hunt. The famous gladiator Paris will fight. Hurrah for Paris! Hurrah for the generous Flaccus, who is running for duumvirate!"

Below is a personal plug for the sign writer reading: "Marcus wrote this sign by the light of the moon. If you hire Marcus, he'll work day and night to do a good job."

It was a fine day and a big crowd turned out that filled the circus. Owners of neighboring houses that overlooked the amphitheater rented out their roof tops to people who couldn't get seats. (Later the Circus Maximus got so high that this source of revenue was lost.) Around the base of the stands the moat of running water kept the arena cool. The crowd had programs to guide them in betting. The programs were written in a sort of sporting code and one of the later ones looked like this:

T.	*M.*
v. Pugnax Ner. III	p. Murranus Ner. III
Ess.	*Ess.*
m. P. Ostorius Jul. LI	v. Scylax Jul. XXVI

This meant that a gladiator named Pugnax, a Thracian (fighting with a small, round shield and short, curved sword) was pitted against Murranus, a Myrmillo (Gallic arms like the Secutor). Both came from the Neroniani School of gladiators founded by Nero at Capua. Both had won three times. (If it was a man's first fight, T for tyro was put after his name.) The "v" and "p" were written in by the owner of the programs later. The *v* stood for victor and the *p* for perished.

The second line meant that Publius Ostorius (apparently a freeman, judging from his double name, who probably fought for hire) and winner in fifty-one fights was opposed to a man named Scylax who had won twenty-six times. Both were from the Julian Gladiatorial School. The "Ess" stands for Essedarii, which means that they fought from chariots. Scylax was the winner but Ostorius' life was spared (possibly because he was a Roman citizen) by the crowd. The "m" stands for "missus" (let go).

After A. Clodius Flaccus had ridden around the arena in his hired chariot, followed by his stooges, there was a parade of the gladiators, each man wearing the armor and carrying the weapons with which he was to fight. Very fine it must have looked, too, the armor flashing in the sun, the feathers in the casques nodding, the powerful gladiators striding along and the fifty-piece band playing a march. The gladiators halted in front of the emperor's private box and, raising their right hands straight out, chanted:

"Hail, Caesar! We who are about to die greet thee!"

Then they turned and in military formation marched out through Porta Libitinensis (a small gate under the stands) to their room.

After a few preliminary bouts of acrobats, trained animals and trick riding, it was time for the fights. The gladiators were mainly matched against a group of German prisoners of war. This was because a highly trained gladiator was a very valuable investment and the lanistae did everything they could to keep the men from getting killed unnecessarily. The best way to safeguard a gladiator was to pit him against a nonprofessional. When gladiator fought gladiator, the match was frequently fixed, at least in this comparatively early period. Even if the mob demanded a fallen man's life, the victor only pretended to kill him. He was then hauled out with a hook as though a corpse and later sent to some provincial circus where he wouldn't be recognized. A lot depended on the editor giving the games. He could insure better fights if he insisted on the men fighting to the death, but that cost extra.

The Germans were armed with their national weapon: short javelins. They had no armor but wore heavy bearskins as protection. However, they outnumbered the gladiators sent against them two to one. Still, the highly trained gladiators didn't have much trouble except with one man. He was a Norseman, a giant with long blond hair and beard. He was fighting with an enormous two-handed sword. He killed two gladiators, cutting off their heads in spite of the gorget that protected their necks. He got such a hand that the fight was stopped and the Norseman promised his freedom. The applause went to his head for he insisted on making a speech to the crowd in broken Latin. The Norseman said that he'd killed six legionnaires in battle before he was captured, that the Romans were all yellow-bellies and one Norseman could handle a legion of them, and that he could personally lick any man in the crowd. The crowd were sportsmen enough to admire his nerve and applauded, but in the stands was a young officer whose father had been killed fighting the Germanic tribes. This fellow didn't like Nordics and he jumped into the arena and challenged the Norseman to fight.

The Norseman accepted and as this was obviously a real grudge match, the crowd was all for it. Not having any arms with him, the officer borrowed Flamma's armor and sword. Then he and the Norseman went to it.

The combatants were so evenly matched that there was none of the usual shouting and cheering from the stands; the crowd held its breath, watching every move. There was no sound in the giant amphitheater but the clash of the swords. In spite of his armor, the young officer had counted on being quicker than the big Norseman in his cumbersome bearskin but the Norseman displayed an amazing and unexpected agility. Twice he beat the

Roman to his knees and only a miracle saved the young man. Then the Roman, leaping back to avoid a stroke from the great two-handed sword, slipped in a pool of blood. He went down and the Norseman straddled him, shortening his sword for the death stroke.

A gasp went up from the crowd, for it was all over now. Suddenly the prone man brought up his shield between the Norseman's legs. As the big man doubled up in agony, the Roman rolled away and, bounding to his feet, plunged his sword into his opponent's armpit where the heavy bearskin did not cover him. The Norseman went down while the crowd screamed in delirious excitement and the band played frenetically.

Naturally, all anyone remembered of that set of games was the young officer's brilliant victory, but Flamma was well content. He had disposed of his two Germans in a neat, businesslike way and as an ex-soldier he had learned to do the job assigned to him and let it go at that. He greatly admired the young officer's feat and was proud that his armor and sword had been used, but he was only a gladiator and that sort of grandstand stuff could well be left to some red-hot young aristocrat with more guts than sense.

The lanista kept his eye on Flamma. He liked the soldier's way of fighting: nothing spectacular, but dependable. In the next few years, Flamma defeated Greek Hoplomachi in full armor and fighting with pikes, Dimachaeri with daggers in each hand and Andabatae on horseback. His usual opponents were Samnites who were equipped much like the Secutors. The Samnites were the first professional gladiators because the big gladiatorial combats began shortly after the Samnite nation was conquered by the Romans and the prisoners were used as gladiators. For a long time, the words "gladiator" and "Samnite" were interchangeable but as Romans conquered other nations, new styles of gladiators were constantly being introduced so the Samnites became simply one type of fighter. However, they never lost their appeal and might be called the "standard gladiator," all other sorts being more or less novelty acts.

Flamma was beaten a few times but was always saved by the crowd, which gave the "thumbs up" signal that meant a fallen man was to be spared. Flamma, winning or losing, always put up a good fight and the crowd liked him.

There has been a lot of discussion exactly as to how the mob signaled their wishes. Until recently it was believed that "thumbs down" was the death signal and "thumbs up" meant the man was to live. Some authorities today think that the death signal was made by stabbing with the thumb at the spectator's own chest meaning "let him have it here" and the signal for release was to extend the hand flat with the thumb bent under the palm. Others think that the thumb was only used to signal death, that if the man was to be released the crowd waved their handkerchiefs. No one knows. Perhaps there were many different gestures and they went by fads; some being popular at one period and others at another.

Not being a flashy fighter, Flamma had a slow publicity build-up but gradually people began to notice the big man who never went in for any grandstand plays but nearly always won. Some fighters put on a regular act like modern wrestlers—taking great swipes at each other, banging their shields around, pretending to fall, staggering as though they had received a mortal wound and then heroically returning to the fray. Again as with wrestling, there was often a "hero" and a "villain." The hero was usually some clean-cut young Roman, often a freeman fighting for hire or some rich young wastrel who had run through his inheritance and turned to the arena as a last resort. The hero always got a careful build-up and was given a big ovation as he explained to the crowd that he was only fighting to get enough money to bury his father or support his widowed mother. The villain was a tough-looking brute who came out yelling insults at the hero, spitting at him, and promising to massacre the bum. The hero always won. Such fights naturally had to be fixed or the gladiatorial schools would have run out of villains.

The fights were by no means always staged. The crowd was pretty shrewd at detecting fakes and also it was hard to persuade a gladiator to throw a fight if he thought he could win because it would be up to his opponent whether to kill him or not, regardless of what previous arrangement might have been made. Still, up to the reign of Tiberius (or, roughly about 20 A.D.) there was a good deal of give and take in the arena. A highly trained gladiator was a valuable man and knew it. An experienced gladiator wouldn't fight a tyro. Many of them openly expressed their contempt of the crowd and used to stop in the middle of a fight to cuss the people out, in the manner of Mr. Leo Durocher. They developed an enormous esprit de corps. A gladiator prided himself on bearing any wound without a cry and even when mortally wounded would shout to the lanista for instructions. The lanista was allowed to stand on the sidelines while his man fought, like a prize fighter's manager, and shout instructions. This was a great help to Flamma, who wasn't too smart and often needed someone to shout: "Try him with an uppercut under the palette" (the shoulder-piece) and so on.

Slowly, by hard work and considerable luck, Flamma worked his way up to being one of the top gladiators in Rome. He never faked a fight, he always did his best, and he gradually won a following in the city. Sculptors made statues of him; his head appeared on coins as Mars, the god of war; he was wined and dined in wealthy homes and given an estate by a rich lady admirer. Crowds of women followed him around and on street walls were scribbled: "Flamma is a girl's sigh and prayer" and "Oh you Flamma! You're the doctor who can cure what's wrong with me." He never did as well as the gladiator Spiculus who was given a palace by Nero, or Veianius whose son was made a knight, but Flamma wasn't complaining. He began to grow rich. After a successful fight, whoever was putting on the games had to present the winning gladiators with a bowl of gold coins, the exact amount being specified by the crowd. Also, like Diocles, Flamma sold tips on the fights, having a good idea which of two gladiators had the best chance of surviving.

At this time, a gladiator had to fight for three years. Then he was excused from actual combat but remained a slave, working at the gladiatorial school for another five. But the crowd could at any time demand that a gladiator be given a wooden sword, which meant that he could retire from the arena. Before the actual combats, the gladiators warmed up by fighting with wooden weapons and so the wooden sword symbolized that in future the man would never have to fight for his life.

After one of his most brilliant fights, the enthusiastic crowd voted Flamma the coveted wooden sword. Flamma refused it indignantly.

"Are you crazy?" he roared at the stands. "I'm making more money than anyone in Rome, I can have any woman I want, I'm living in a villa and I'm the toast of the empire. Leave the arena? What for?"

"Good old Flamma!" howled the delighted crowd. Flamma refused the proffered wooden sword four times, the only gladiator who ever turned down this offer not once but several times over. As a result, his name has come down to us over nearly two thousand years.

When he finally retired, he was given an ivory rectangle, like a G.I.'s dogtag, to wear around his neck. It was inscribed with his name, the name of his former owner, and the date on which he was set free. Flamma married and lived to a gray old age in his villa, telling everyone who'd listen that the modern gladiators didn't have the stuff the boys did when he was a young man. When he died, his devoted family had the record of his victories carved on his tomb.

Flamma's attitude toward his profession was not unique. A Myrmillo, during a period when fights were few, was heard to complain that he was wasting the best years of his life. Epictetus, a Roman writer, says that the gladiators used to pray for more fights so that they could distinguish themselves in the arena and make more money. (Not too surprising, when the famous toast of the armed forces in Great Britain used to be: "Here's to a sudden plague and bloody war!"—the only two events that could speed up promotion.)

Although never nearly as popular as the sword fights, boxing was also featured in the arena. It was originally simply an athletic event as with our college boxing, and then the promoters decided to liven it up to appeal to the crowd. The leather straps over the knuckles were studded with leadlike brass knuckles. These devices were called "caestus" and later were even equipped with nails. The caestus of a famous fighter, covered with blood and brains, were hung up in one school to encourage young hopefuls.

Statius gives this description of a boxing match. The editor opens the fight by shouting:

"'Now courage is needed. Use the terrible caestus in close fighting—next to using swords, this is the best way to test your bravery.'

"Capaneus put on the raw oxhide straps covered with lumps of lead—and he was as hard as the lead. His opponent comes out, a young, curly-haired boy named Alcidamas. Capaneus takes one look at him, laughs and shouts, 'Haven't you anybody better than that?' They lift their arms, deadly as thunderbolts, watching each other. Capaneus is a giant but getting old. Alcidamas is only a youth but stronger than he looks.

"They spar, feeling each other out, just touching their gloves. Then Capaneus moves in and starts slugging, but Alcidamas holds him off and Capaneus only tires his arms and hurts his own chances. The young fellow, a smart fighter, parries, ducks, leans back and bends his head forward to avoid the swings. He turns the blows with his gloves and advances with his feet while keeping his head well back. Capaneus is stronger and has a terrific right but young Alcidamas, feinting right and left, distracts him and then getting his right hand above the older man, comes down from on top. He gets home on his forehead. The blood runs.

"Capaneus doesn't realize how badly he's hurt but he hears the yelling of the crowd and stopping to wipe the sweat off his face with the back of his glove, he sees the blood. Now he really gets mad and goes for the boy.

"His blows are wasted on the air; most of them only hit his opponent's gloves and the boy stays away from him, running backward but hitting when he gets a chance.

"Capaneus chases him around the arena until both of them are too tired to move and they stand panting and facing each other. Then Capaneus makes a wild dash. Alcidamas dodges and hits him on the shoulder. Capaneus goes down! He falls on his head and tries to get up but the boy knocks him down again. Suddenly Capaneus jumps up and goes at the boy, flailing with both fists. The boy falls and Capaneus bends over him, hammering him on the head. The crowd yells, 'Save the poor kid! His skull's cracked already and Capaneus is going to beat his brains out.' The attendants rush in and pull Capaneus off his victim. 'You've won!' they tell him. Capaneus bellows, 'Let me go! I'll smash his face in! I'll spoil that pretty fairy's good looks that make him so damned popular with the crowd.' The attendants had to drag him out of the arena."

Not surprisingly, the old-type circus acts consisting of acrobats, tumblers and animal trainers had a tough time competing with the gladiators and chariot races. One after another they began to drop out and it looked as though they'd be dead as vaudeville. But one man by the name of Ursus Togatus resolved not to be beaten by a bunch of plug-uglies and horses. Ursus could shoot a bow and arrow with his toes while standing on his hands, juggle five glass balls, and had a troupe of trained bears that acted out a play while dressed in clothes. Pretty tame stuff, but he must have been well liked at one time, as he had his picture painted on vases as a souvenir of the circus. He was a tall man with abnormally long arms and legs. He seems a trifle pudgy but apparently he was limber enough. He had a long, clean-shaven face and looked like an exceptionally clever horse.

Ursus was one of the few people in show business who was ever able to adapt himself to a new trend and he made circus history. He dropped his juggling and instead of a troupe of performing bears he kept only one—a really tough animal. When the bear charged him, Togatus would run at the animal with a long pole, vault over his back and race for the arena wall. With the bear right at his heels, he'd use his impetus to run up the wall, jump over the bear again, and then tear back to his pole and repeat the performance. The crowd loved the act, as there was always a good chance that Togatus wouldn't make it.

Other animal trainers quickly got the idea. One man walked on stilts through a pack of hungry hyenas. Another rolled around the arena in a large openwork metal ball while three lions tried to get at him. One of them finally succeeded in tearing his arm off through a hole in the ball but other performers copied the act. Acrobatic troupes of men and women learned how to grab a charging bull by the horns and turn somersaults over its back. The Romans liked animal acts, especially if they were dangerous, so in spite of the gladiators there were always animals in the circus.

By 50 B.C., the exhibitions were rough enough, heaven knows, but they were still fairly well controlled and on a comparatively modest scale. But in 46 B.C., a victorious general named Julius Caesar with political ambitions arrived in Rome. In spite of his triumphs, Julius was in the doghouse both with the Senate and the people. They suspected him of wanting to be a dictator. Cicero warned him, "You are only a dwarf tied to a long sword. You have the army but the people will never tolerate you."

Caesar smiled. "Sulla, the dictator, tried to subdue the people by force and failed. I have other plans."

Caesar knew the Roman mob. He put on the first of the really big shows in Roman history, rebuilding the Circus Maximus to hold them. There was a hunt of four hundred lions, fights between elephants and infantry, evening parades of elephants carrying lighted torches in their trunks, bull fighting by mounted Thessalians and the first giraffes ever seen in Rome (Cleopatra sent him the giraffes as a present). The chariot races alone lasted for ten days, from dawn to dark. There were also gladiatorial combats—how many isn't recorded but the senators were so horrified that they passed a law limiting the number of gladiators any one man could own to three hundred and twenty pairs. Caesar may have had a couple of thousand—practically a small army. He used them as a bodyguard when they weren't fighting in the arena.

The law limiting the ownership of gladiators didn't last long. The people went mad over these big games and didn't care if

Caesar became dictator or not as long as he kept them amused. But by now, a number of prominent men felt that the games were getting to be a danger. The people would elect anyone to office who gave them a good show. A group of wealthy men decided to give the public more educational entertainment. They hired a troupe of famous Greek actors to perform some of the great classical plays. In the middle of the first performance, a man rushed into the theater to say that some gladiators were fighting in the circus. In ten minutes, the Greek actors were playing to an empty hours. After that the reformers gave up.

Although Caesar had staged the games simply as a popularity getter, they gave him an idea. He said to Dolabella, one of his top advisors, "This is a perfect way to try out new weapons and fighting techniques. Our legions will be fighting tribes from all over the world. Let's pit captives from different tribes against each other, each using his own weapons."

This opened up a whole new era in the games. Not just a few professional gladiators fought but whole battles were staged. Tattooed Britons fighting from chariots went out against German tribesmen; Africans with shields and spears took on Arabs fighting from horseback with bows and arrows. Thracians who used scimitars and had little, rough shields strapped to their left wrists engaged the heavily armed Samnites. Once the entire arena was planted to resemble a forest, and a company of legionnaires, condemned to the circus for various military misdemeanors, had to march through it while Gauls in their native costume and with their native weapons, ambushed them. An engagement was staged between war elephants and cavalry to get the horses accustomed to the big animals. Meanwhile, Caesar and his general staff sat in the imperial box and took notes. The winning side was generally given its freedom, which insured a good fight.

Julius Caesar might be called the father of the games because under him they ceased to be an occasional exhibition of fairly modest proportions and became a national institution. By the time of Augustus, the people regarded the games not as a luxury but as their right. Under the old Republic, the games lasted for sixteen days: fourteen chariot races, two trials for horses, and forty-eight theatricals. By the time of Claudius (50 A.D.), there were ninety-three a year. This number was gradually increased to a hundred and twenty-three days under Trajan and to two hundred and thirty under Marcus Aurelius. Eventually there were games of some kind or other going on all the time. In 248 A.D. the crowd didn't go to bed for three days and nights. Augustus and several of the other emperors tried to limit the number but it always produced mob uprisings. Marcus Aurelius disliked the games but in his official position had to attend, like a president opening the baseball season by throwing out the first ball. He used to sit in the royal box and dictate letters to his secretaries while the games were going on. The mob never forgave him, any more than a modern crowd would forgive a president who sat transacting official business with the bases loaded and Mickey Mantle at bat. Marcus Aurelius was one of the best emperors Rome ever had but as a result of his contempt for the games, he was also one of the most unpopular.

Claudius, who was probably insane, was very popular. He loved the games and used to make a great point of pretending to add up the betting odds on his fingers (although he was an excellent mathematician) as did the crowd. He also used to jump into the arena to berate the gladiators for not fighting hard enough, send people in the crowd notes asking what they thought of some particular gladiator's chances, and tell dirty jokes. Both Caligula and Nero, probably the two worst rulers in history, were greatly mourned by the crowd because they always put on such magnificent games. Nero, who used to light the arena at night by crucifying Christians and then setting fire to their oil-soaked bodies, was especially beloved. Even after he was forced to kill himself by the Praetorian Guard, the people refused to believe that he was dead. For years opportunists kept cropping up, claiming to be Nero, and always got a following of people who remembered what wonderful games the insane emperor had provided.

III

The demand of the crowd, not only for bigger and better games but also for novelties, kept increasing and the government was hard put to it not only to provide elaborate enough spectacles but also to think up new displays. Possibly the most elaborate demonstrations of all were the naumachia or naval combats. Julius Caesar originated these displays in 46 B.C., digging a special lake in Mars' Field on the outskirts of Rome for the show. Sixteen galleys manned by four thousand rowers and two thousand fighting men fought to the finish. This spectacle was later surpassed by Augustus in 2 B.C. He had a permanent lake built for these fights, measuring 1800 feet long by 1200 feet wide, on the far side of the Tiber River. Marble stands were constructed around the lake for the crowd. Traces of this gigantic construction project still remain. One engagement was between two fleets of twelve ships each with crews of three thousand men (besides the rowers), to commemorate the Battle of Salamis. The men on the opposing fleets were dressed like Greeks and Persians. Later, Titus gave a naumachia on a lake that could be planked over. On the first day, gladiators fought on the planking. On the second, there were chariot races. On the third, the planking was removed and a sea fight took place, in which 3,000 men were engaged.

The greatest naumachia of all time was the naval engagement staged by Claudius. As Augustus' lake was too small, the mad emperor decided to use the Fucine Lake (now called the Lago di Fucino) some sixty miles to the east of Rome. This lake had no natural outlet and in the spring it often flooded many miles of surrounding county. To overcome this trouble, a tunnel three and a half miles long had been cut through solid rock from the lake to the Litis River to carry off the surplus water. This job had taken thirty thousand men eleven years to finish. For the dedication of the opening of this tunnel, Claudius decided to stage a fight between two navies on the lake. The galleys previously used in such engagements had been small craft with only one bank of oars. For this fight, there were to be twenty-four triremes (three banks of oars), all regulation ocean-going warships, and twenty-six biremes (double bank). This armada was divided into two fleets of twenty-five ships each and manned by nineteen hundred criminals under the command of two famous gladiators. One fleet was to represent the Rhodians and the other the Sicilians and both groups wore the appropriate costumes.

Nineteen hundred desperate and well-armed men could be a dangerous force if they decided to band together and turn against the crowd, so the lake was surrounded by heavily armed troops. In addition, a number of regiments were put on rafts equipped with catapults so they could sink the galleys if necessary. The hills around the lake formed a natural amphitheater and on the morning of the fight the slopes were covered with over 500,000 spectators. As the lake was several hours' trip from Rome, the crowd brought their lunches and picnicked while watching the fight.

Fortunately, it turned out to be a nice day. As the lake was nearly two hundred square miles in size, the fight was restricted to the southwestern section, the rafts being lashed together to form a semicircle across the lake and mark the limits for maneuvering. The Emperor Claudius sat on a specially prepared dais in a superb suit of golden armor covered with a purple cloak, while the Queen Mother, Agrippina, in a mantle of cloth of gold, sat beside him. In addition to the infantry surrounding the lake, there was also a detachment of cavalry mounted on magnificent Sicilian steeds drawn up behind the royal family. In order to handle the mob, the slopes had been divided into sections, each section under the care of a magistrate. A big tent had even been put up to care for the wounded after the battle— after all, prisoners were scarce and the survivors could always be used again in other spectacles. As matters turned out, the tent served another purpose. Fifteen women in the crowd gave birth during the fight and had to be cared for in the tent. It is an interesting example of the mob's passion for these fights that women in advanced pregnancy traveled sixty miles from Rome so as not to miss the naumachia.

The signal for the onslaught was given by a silver Triton that rose from the lake and blew on a golden conch shell. This mechanical contrivance must have taken some doing but it was nothing to many of the tricks that the Romans were able to dream up. If they had expended the same amount of skill and ingenuity in improving their weapons, Rome might never have fallen. At the conch-shell signal, the two fleets approached the royal dais: drums beating, trumpets blowing and the crews saluting with their weapons.

The triremes were about a hundred feet long, each equipped with an iron beak or ram in the bow. In the bow was reared up a long beam with a spike on one end and the other end fastened to the foredeck by a heavy hinge. This was the corvus or "crow." When the corvus was dropped on an opposing galley, the spike sank into wood and held the two ships together. It could then be used as a gangplank for boarders. The ships carried a single square sail which was effective only if the wind was dead astern. Julius Caesar records how astonished he was when he saw the Venetii ships tack but for some reason or other it never occurred to the Romans that this maneuver might be handy for a sailing ship and they never changed their galleys' rig.

As a result, the galleys depended almost entirely on their oars. The rowers were not in the holds of the galleys but sat on a sort of superstructure projecting over the ships' sides. This was to give the men greater leverage with the oars, for moving one of those big ships even with fifty rowers must have been a tough job. There was one man to an oar and they sat at different levels so the oar blades wouldn't interfere with each other. In the stern sat a man who gave the rowers the time with a drum and two overseers with whips walked up and down platforms running fore and aft to make sure everyone was doing his best. The ships were built long and narrow for speed and were very unseaworthy craft, although they were ideal for a battle on a lake. They were almost identical with the Greek galleys of a thousand years before. All the Romans added, except for the corvus, were foot ropes for the men to stand on while reefing the sail, and shrouds so they could climb the mast. The Greeks had to use a ladder.

The combined fleets passed in review and as they came within hearing distance of the royal dais, the men gave the traditional cry of "Hail, Caesar, we who are about to die greet thee!" Claudius shouted back gaily, "That depends on you, my friends," meaning that if a man put up a good fight he wouldn't be killed. However, the crews yelled, "Good Caesar! If it depends on us, we won't bother to fight." Then the two fleets sailed away together, the crews shouting congratulations to each other.

The mob howled protests and Claudius, jumping off his throne, ran down to the shore, yelling insults at the crews and swearing to have the soldiers set fire to the ships and burn them alive if they didn't fight. Claudius was crippled (he may have been a polio victim) and was also weak in the head. He used to go into insane rages and this was a typical one. The crowd laughed themselves sick at his antics but finally the crews got the idea and, dividing into two fleets, made ready for the battle. Agrippina led the emperor back to his throne where Claudius, seeing the crowd laugh, began to laugh too, and got hysterical.

When the royal family finally got Claudius quieted down, he gave the signal for the fight by dropping his handkerchief. Instantly the war trumpets of both fleets blared out and the galleys began to move, the drummers building up the stroke as rapidly as possible, for it was of vital importance for the ships to have the maximum amount of momentum when they met.

When galleys fought, they first tried to ram each other with the iron beaks in the prows. If this maneuver succeeded, the rammed galley sank within a few minutes and nothing more needed to be done. If the ramming failed, then each galley tried to plow through the oars of the enemy. As the oars were forced back, the handles crushed the rowers at their benches and the disabled galley could then be rammed at leisure. If this maneuver also failed, then there was nothing for it but to board with the aid of the corvus and slug it out man to man.

On the first onslaught, nine of the Rhodian galleys were sunk by ramming and three of the Sicilian. Many of the Rhodian galleys had lost one or more banks of oars and could not maneuver. They managed to crowd together at one end of the lake and the Sicilian fleet surrounded them and attacked by boarding. The fight, which had started at ten in the morning, went on until three in the afternoon. The Sicilian triremes put up a desperate resistance, Tacitus saying: "The battle, though between malefactors, was fought with the spirit of brave men." Several of the Sicilian single-banked galleys, however, did their best to keep out of the fight. At last "when the surface of the lake was red with blood," the last of the Sicilian fleet surrendered. Three thousand men were killed. The fight had been so exciting that Claudius pardoned the survivors on both sides except for the crews of the three Rhodian galleys who had been rammed, because he thought that they hadn't charged into the fight fast enough, and the crews of six of the Sicilian single-banked galleys, who had been gold-bricking.

This exhibition was such a success that four months later, Claudius gave another show. As he was fresh out of prisoners (all the Roman jails had been swept clean to provide crews for the galleys) he had to be content with a less elaborate production. This time he had a bridge on pontoons stretched across the lake, widening in the middle to a platform about a hundred yards wide. Two armies of about five thousand men each were raised from prisoners of war, newly arrived jailbirds, and slaves. One was dressed up like Etruscans and the other as Samnites. Each side was given the appropriate arms, all the Etruscans weapons having to be made especially for the event as the Etruscans had ceased to exist as a nation three hundred years before. However, some of the old Etruscans' double-headed battle-axes and bronze lances were still in museums and these were carefully duplicated by the Roman smiths.

While the bands played, the two armies marched across the bridge from opposite sides of the lake and met in the middle. Claudius had given orders that no one was to be allowed to swim ashore. If he fell off the bridge, he had either to drown or climb back. At first the Samnites seemed to be winning, pushing the Etruscans back and holding the wide central part of the bridge. But the Etruscans rallied and finally drove the Samnites off the span. All the Etruscans, and a few of the Samnites who had shown outstanding courage, were given their freedom.

IV

The first century of the Christian era probably marked the high point of the games. The spectacles had grown to such an extent that it seemed incredible that they could ever be surpassed. The dictator Sulla (93 B.C.) had exhibited one hundred lions in the arena. Julius Caesar had four hundred. Pompey had six hundred lions, twenty elephants and 410 leopards which fought Gaetulians armed with darts. Augustus in 10 A.D. exhibited the first tiger ever to be seen in Rome and had 3,500 elephants. He boasted that he had ten thousand men killed in eight shows. After Trajan's victory over the Dacians, he had eleven thousand animals killed in the arena. The cost of the games also steadily increased. In 364 B.C., the total cost of the games was $10,725. In 51 A.D., they cost $92,530.* This was the sum paid by the emperor; no record has been kept of the games put on by private individuals or politicians, but Petronius speaks of a magistrate who was going to spend $20,000 on a three-day show to keep him in office.

The buildings designed to hold these shows have never been surpassed either for size or for perfection of functional design.

---

* I am computing the Roman sesterce as having the purchasing power of about 25 cents today.

The oldest and largest of these vast structures was the Circus Maximus. Although I've described what the arena looked like I haven't said much about the building itself. It was built in the Vallis Murcia, a long valley between the Palatine and Aventine Hills which had been used for chariot races from remote antiquity. Eventually wooden stands, which could be removed after the races were put up on the slopes of the hills for the audience. The first permanent stands were put up in 329 B.C. together with stalls for the chariots. Only the first tier of seats was of stone; the rest continued to be wood. As a result, the stadium was burned down several times, one of the times being when Nero burned Rome. After each burning, it was rebuilt with fresh splendor. Julius Caesar enlarged it to such an extent that some historians date the true Circus Maximus from his time. Caesar put in a ten-foot moat which protected the people from the wild beasts in the arena. A stream was diverted from the hills to feed this moat and still runs near the Via di Cerchi. Augustus is generally given credit for having completed the circus although later emperors continued to enlarge the building. Claudius had the wooden chariot stalls replaced by marble and the cones made of gilt bronze. During the time of Antonius Pius, the stands were so crowded that the upper wooden tiers collapsed, killing 1,112 people. As a result, the stadium was rebuilt completely of stone. Trajan covered the whole building with white marble inside and out, relieved with gold trim work and paintings. He also added columns of colored Oriental marble and statues of marble and gilt bronze. Eventually the Circus Maximus came to measure 2,000 feet long by 650 feet wide and held 385,000 people—a quarter of the population of Rome.

Constantine gave the circus three additional tiers of marble seats supported on concrete arches. These arches still remain and form part of the foundation for the church of Saint

Anastasia. They were made seven feet thick to support the great weight of the stands. The circus continued to exist through the Middle Ages but was used as a vast quarry, and many of the early churches in Rome were built with stone taken from it. As late as the sixteenth century part of the structure still stood but now only the site and a few of the seats can be seen.

The Colosseum, started by the Emperor Vespasian in 70 A.D. and completed by his son, Titus, ten years later, was the most perfectly equipped amphitheater that the Romans or anyone else ever built. As Vespasian and Titus were members of the Flavian family, it was known to the Romans as the "Flavian amphitheater" and it wasn't until the Middle Ages that it was called the Colosseum because of its size. Unlike the Circus Maximus (which was open at one end), the Colosseum formed a complete oval. It measures 615 by 510 feet and the arena alone is 281 by 177 feet. It covers six acres. Archaeologists think it could hold about 50,000 spectators although the Romans claimed that 100,000 people saw the shows, packed into the aisles. (Madison Square Garden in New York holds 18,903.) Its walls originally rose 160 feet high and may have been topped by wooden seats as bleachers. The arena could be flooded for sea fights. It was equipped with a system of elevators, raised and lowered by counter-weights and pulleys, which brought up the wild beasts from their underground cages to the arena at the right moment. Even today, when two-thirds of the building are gone, it remains one of the most impressive structures in the world.

The building has eighty entrances; seventy-six were used by the general public while one was reserved for the emperor and one for the Vestal Virgins, a group of chief priestesses whose duty was to guard a sacred flame which was kept burning continuously. The other two doors opened directly into the arena. One was called the Door of Life and through it the opening procession marched before the show. The other was called the Door of Death and through it the dead bodies of men and beasts were dragged to clear the arena for the next event.

Ivory tickets were distributed for the shows, each one marked with a seat number, tier number and entrance number. Under the stands was an elaborate system of passageways and ramps so that when you entered the building you were able to go directly to your seat with a minimum of trouble. The stands were divided horizontally by flat walks (praecinctiones) and vertically by stairs (cunei). The seats were made of marble, numbered, and with lines inscribed on the marble showing the limits of each seat. Marble diagrams with the seating arrangements marked on them were set in the walls by the entrances. One is now in the Capitoline Museum in Rome. There were four tiers of seats, the three lowest represented on the outside of the building by a circle of arches which admitted light and air into the passageways. The topmost tier has now virtually disappeared. The arches of the ground level tier were used as entrances. The arches of the next two tiers contained statues of the gods, all except the arches directly above the two main entrances which were bigger than the rest and held life-sized representations of a chariot with four horses and the driver. The first three tiers each had columns of a different type and the topmost tier was solid masonry with forty small windows flanked by ornamental columns set in the masonry.

An elaborate series of sewers carried off the blood and refuse from the arena and the animal cages below it. A system of small sewers led from all parts of the building to one great circular drain which surrounded the Colosseum. This drain, in turn, connected to the Cloaca Maxima, the main sewerage system of the city.

Around the inside of the arena ran a perfectly smooth marble wall about fifteen feet high made of carefully jointed blocks so no animal could climb it. Directly above this wall was the podium, a flat area about fifteen feet wide where the emperor had his box and the nobility sat, composed of senators, knights and the civil and military tribunes. There were apparently no permanent seats on the podium. As in modern boxes, the seats (called curale) were movable and the occupants could stand and walk around as they wished. The podium was separated from the first tier of seats by a low wall. In this first tier sat the rich merchants and minor officials. After that, came the ordinary people.

As a leopard can jump fifteen feet and a tiger can jump twenty, the podium wall was obviously not enough to protect the spectators. However, elephant tusks about five feet long were fixed to the edge of the podium and nets strung along them in such a way that they overhung the arena. In addition, a bronze bar ran along the top of the wall that turned on a pivot so if an animal did jump high enough to grab the bar, it would turn and drop him back into the arena. There was also a moat as in the Circus Maximus. The moat was mainly to break the force of an elephant charge. Without such protection, elephants could easily reach the nobility in the podium—as was discovered when Pompey first exhibited elephants in the Circus Maximus in 55 B.C. before Julius Caesar had the moat dug. Iron gratings had been put up for additional protection but the elephants ripped these down and only fast footwork on the part of the emperor and his friends saved their lives.

These precautions might seem enough but most authorities believe that there was also an inner wall of heavy wooden planks running around the arena about ten feet from the podium wall and that the moat lay between this inner barrier and the central part of the arena. There are several reasons for believing this inner wall existed. The Colosseum was so vast that there must have been some way of keeping the animals out in the middle of the arena and away from the podium wall—otherwise the people in the two upper tiers of seats couldn't have seen them because the edge of the podium would have cut off the view. The natural instinct of a wild animal turned loose in a brightly lighted arena full of shouting, yelling people is to hug the wall, and scattered references by Roman writers show that the animals in the Colosseum often did just that. They were driven away from the wall by arena slaves using hot irons or burning straw but there are no openings in the podium wall through which the slaves could have reached the animals. Also, there are many references to the elaborate scenic effects which acted as backdrops for the shows; the animals issuing from artificial caves, gladiators fighting before a painting representing ancient Carthage, and so on. It is hard to see how this scenery could have been erected and taken down if it were hung on the podium wall, especially as the changes often had to be made while the arena was full of wild animals and certainly the slaves were not allowed on the podium itself among the noble onlookers.

All these facts suggest that there must have been an inner wall, probably made of heavy planks fastened to poles set into the floor of the arena. The elephant tusks carrying the overhang nets may have been fastened to these poles rather than to the podium wall itself. This inner wall could be painted, or have painted canvases hung on it, representing any scene desired. It may not always have been a board fence but composed of artificial rocks made of lathes and plaster, tree trunks to represent a forest or any other material that the stage designers of the Colosseum decided to use. The slaves who changed the scenery could operate between the podium wall and this inner barrier. The barrier must have joined the podium wall at the Gate of Life and the Gate of Death. The overhanging nets couldn't be used at these two places but Calpurnius says that revolving ivory wheels were set into the podium wall at these points to keep the animals from climbing it.

There must have been at least a circle of tall masts in the arena itself, for the great awning which covered the top of the Colosseum to protect the audience from sun and rain had to be supported in the center by some means. We know that around the top of the Colosseum ran a circle of 240 masts (the sockets where they stood can still be seen) and these masts held the edge of the awning. However, unless the Romans had some very ingenious method for keeping the awning taut, there must have been masts coming up from the arena to take the weight of the great mass in the center. There may even have been wooden catwalks running across the top of the Colosseum under this awning, as on a modern Hollywood sound stage, for the ancient writers talk of naked little boys with wings tied to them to represent cupids being swung back and forth across the arena by invisible wires as though they were flying. Often large animals, in one case a bull, were carried up to the awning (which was painted to represent the sky) by invisible wires to illustrate some mythological incident. To make such stunts as this possible, there must have been platforms at the top of the building equipped with blocks and tackles as well as space for crews of highly trained stagehands. Yet no matter how complicated were the mechanical miracles that these men had to produce, there was seldom a hitch in the performance. If there was, the stagehands were thrown into the arena to be eaten by wild beasts or killed by gladiators.

The games were worked on a very tight schedule and something had to be going on every minute or the crowd became restless. Anyone who has ever had any connection with a modern circus knows what a tremendous problem it is to get the various acts, especially the animal acts, on and off on time. The Romans were working with wild animals and condemned criminals so their problem was incredibly complicated. They were also operating on a gigantic scale—the games often ran for a couple of months and sometimes five thousand animals were in the arena at the same time. Getting such a huge number of animals out of their cages and into the arena must have been a fantastic job.

We have a pretty good idea how the Romans did it from studying the honeycomb of passages under the arena. The Romans used at least four systems. The cages could be dragged up to the arena on a series of ramps and then put into niches under the podium wall. At a given signal, all the doors were opened simultaneously and at the same time slaves dropped burning straw into the backs of the cages through slots in the top specially provided for this purpose. If there was an inner wall, the animals must have reached it by runways as lions enter the big cage in a modern circus. Or perhaps the cages were only kept in the podium niches so they'd be ready when the time came. As soon as the previous act—chariot racing, gladiators or whatever—was finished, the cages were quickly pulled from their niches in the podium wall, dragged to openings in the inner barrier, and opened there.

Another method, probably used with less dangerous animals than the big cats, was to turn them loose in a passageway leading to the arena and then force them on with a movable wooden barrier that just fitted across the passage. There were catches on the sides of the barrier that fitted into holes on the walls so the barrier couldn't be pushed back. These holes can still be seen.

Still another method was to put the animals into an elevator and take them directly up to the floor of the arena. There were a number of these elevators placed at various spots in the arena like trapdoors on a modern stage. The elevator went down into a deep well, the animals were driven onto it, and then the platform was hoisted to arena level by pulleys. In some cases, "breakaway" cages were used that would fall to pieces when certain pins were released. These cages were carried out into the arena, the pins jerked clear, and the animals left exposed as the sides of the cages fell to the ground. The Romans also had cages that operated on the same principle as the chutes used in rodeos; that is, the two sides were hinged so that they could be swung back parallel with the rear leaving the animal completely exposed. All these devices were necessary as it is almost impossible to induce a frightened animal to leave its cage under normal conditions.

In addition to the problems of handling the animals, the arena might in the course of a day's show be flooded for a sea fight and then planted to represent a forest. This might be followed by the erection of an artificial mountain complete with streams, bushes and growing flowers, which then had to be cleared for chariot races and immediately afterwards a gigantic fight might be staged representing Hannibal's attack on Rome—including elephants and catapults plus a mock city defended by condemned legionnaires. Thousands of slaves must have been employed in these great spectacles and every last one of them trained to split-second timing. The sailors from the fleet were used to raise and lower the great awning as these were the only men with sufficient training to handle vast spreads of cloth. The places where the awning lines chafed the stone walls still show.

V

By the time the Colosseum was built, wild animal shows were an important part of the games. Wild beasts had always appeared in the shows from the earliest days, either in the form of trained animal acts or for hunts in which deer, wild goats and antelopes were turned loose in the arena and killed by experienced hunters. Later dangerous animals such as lions, leopards, wild boars and tigers were introduced and gladiators sent out to kill them. Augustus had a bandit named Selurus dropped into a cage of wild beasts and this sight made such a hit that the execution of condemned prisoners by wild animals became a regular part of the shows. So many elaborate and ingenious uses were made of wild animals (which were particularly popular with the mob while the upper classes preferred the gladiatorial contests) that a special class of men called bestiarii were created to handle the animal turns. These men had their own school as did the gladiators and had their own traditions, professional slang and uniform.

One of these bestiarii was named Carpophorus. We know of him because the poet Martial wrote enthusiastically, "Carpophorus could have handled the hydra, the chimaera and the fire-eating bulls at the same time." That's all we know about Carpophorus. Let's describe a top bestiarii during the reign of the Emperor Domitian, shortly after the building of the Colosseum. We'll call our hero Carpophorus for convenience's sake.

Carpophorus, we'll suppose, was a freeman. He was the son of freed slaves who had died, leaving the boy destitute. As his parents had been freed, the boy was also free but as the son of former slaves, he was regarded with contempt by the Roman mob. Because of this prejudice, finding a job was even harder for him than for most people of his time and at an early age the boy took to hanging around the Circus Maximus, the Circus Flaminius, the Circus Neronis and all the other big and little circuses in Rome of the period, including traveling shows that set up wherever they could find an open spot and featured a few worn-out gladiators and some moth-eaten lions. Little Carpophorus carried water for the elephants, cleaned the cages, polished the gladiators' armor and ran errands for a few copper pieces and his meals.

At night he slept under the arches of the Circus Maximus. There were hundreds of these arches supporting the tiers of seats above and they formed a maze of interlocking passages, holes, runways, and narrow slits where only a boy could crawl. Carpophorus learned to know the whole tangle blindfolded. This "under the stands" was a world of its own inhabited by fortunetellers, astrologers, fruit and souvenir sellers, sausage and hamburg vendors, and prostitutes. All these people formed a close-knit fraternity of their own and made their living out of the crowds going to see the shows. People in the stands who got bored with the games would leave their seats and stroll down to this underground world where they could buy special dishes at the various stands, get a skin of wine, watch Syrian and Moorish women do obscene dances to the music of drums, cymbals and castanets, or engage the services of the plump, highly painted little boys who went around with their smocks hitched up above buttocks.

In this world, Carpophorus grew up. Although he had dreamed at one time of being a famous gladiator and at another of being a great charioteer, his real talent was always with animals. He picked up a couple of stray dogs in the streets and taught them to dance on their hind legs, walk a tightrope, howl dismally when asked, "What do you think of the Red, White, and Blue teams?" and bark enthusiastically when asked, "What do you think of the Greens?" This, of course, if the onlooker was wearing a green flower or scarf. As the dogs obeyed secret hand signals rather than the words, they could be made to bark or whine on whatever color Carpophorus wished.

The boy grew up with few illusions about his job, the Roman mob, or the emperor himself. On one occasion, he carried wine and bread for the arena carpenters while they worked on a magnificent galley so cleverly contrived that by pulling a single dowel the entire ship would fall to pieces. It was supposed that this galley was for one of the shows—in fact, such a galley had been employed in a spectacle only a few weeks before and the Emperor Nero had been deeply interested in it—but on completion the galley was taken to the port of Baiae. A month later it was learned that the queen mother, Agrippina, had been given a splendid new galley by her devoted son, the emperor, which had unaccountably come to pieces in the middle of the bay. Some of the stage carpenters who gossiped ended in the arena. Carpophorus kept his mouth shut but this incident confirmed the boy's belief that the entire world was like the arena—a place without justice or mercy, where only the smart and ruthless could survive.

Later, Carpophorus got a job as helper to some of the

bestiarii in the circus and learned their techniques of handling dangerous wild animals. Once when a bestiarius was trying to drive a bear from the arena, using a sort of cat-o'-nine-tails with lead balls on the ends of the lashes, the bear had turned on him and grabbed the man by the shoulder. Young Carpophorus ran into the arena with a twist of blazing straw snatched from the hand of an arena slave and drove the bear off. Rumors of this feat reached one of the instructors at the School of Bestiarii and he had a talk with the boy. He agreed to send Carpophorus through the school if the boy would agree to serve him as a slave for the next ten years. Carpophorus accepted this offer and so became an auctorati (bound over). He spent two years at the school, learning how to handle animals ranging in size from foxes to elephants.

Although everyone at the school admired the tough young man's uncanny ability with animals, Carpophorus was extremely unpopular and not even the most farsighted of his instructors imagined that the quiet, rather sullen youth would some day be the top bestiarius in Rome. The boy was short, dark, heavy-set, and if not actually clumsy, at least not graceful. A good bestiarius was supposed to be slender and agile like a modern matador. The boy was not a good mixer. His early life had made him suspicious of people—one of the reasons why he had turned to animals with such a passionate intensity— and he had cultivated a chip-on-the-shoulder attitude which his fellow students resented. Carpophorus, on the other hand, regarded them as a lot of amateurs. Most of them had never been in an arena with a wild animal before they came to the school while Carpophorus had been handling wild stock since he was a kid. He didn't think much of his instructors, either, they put too much emphasis on book-learning, always quoting Aristotle and Pliny. Neither of these two learned gentlemen, as far as Carpophorus was concerned, knew beans about animals. They thought a mare could conceive if a south wind blew under her tail. Carpophorus knew better than that.

The boy went through the usual course at the school and learned many things which his rough-and-ready, rule-of-thumb education as cageboy in the arena had not taught him. As with gladiators, there were many types of bestiarii: men who specialized in keeping ahead of the beasts by running, men who learned how to dodge them, bull-fighters, lion-tamers, pole-vaulters, and so on. Carpophorus, because of his great strength and brutal technique, was made a venator—a hunter. He learned how to fight wild animals barehanded, strangling them or breaking their necks. He learned how to blind a lioness by throwing a cape over her head and then cracking her back by striking the loins with the edge of his hand. (At least, the Roman writers claim that bestiarii could do this—it must have been quite a trick.) He also fought bears with a veil in one hand to distract the animal and a sword in the other.

To learn how to dodge, the young man was sent out against a leopard tied to a bull by a long rope. As the bull could move as well as the leopard, this was a far tougher job than if the cat were simply tied to a stake but much easier than if the leopard were free. Another bestiarius with a spear stood behind the animals, goading them on. Carpophorus was also exposed to two wild animals at the same time, such as a lion and a leopard, and had to learn to avoid both. He was sometimes forced to lie on the ground while a wild boar or bull was set on him. Carpophorus had to learn how to leap to his feet at the last instant to escape the rush. He had to learn how to irritate wild animals by allowing them almost to catch him and then vaulting over a low fence or behind a wooden shield (as in modern bullfights). The purpose of this maneuver was to make the animals so furious that they would willingly attack the condemned criminals afterwards thrown to them.

Naturally, Carpophorus was soon covered with scars, but like all bestiarii he was as proud of his scars as a soldier is of his medals, considering them a hallmark of his profession. You could point to any scar and Carpophorus could tell you when and how he had received it.

The young bestiarius had two serious vices: he was a heavy drinker and had a berserk temper. Wine was forbidden the students, except during meals, and then mixed with water, but Carpophorus knew his way around and managed to get his own supply. One of his jobs in the school was to train a leopard to be a man-eater. This was a complicated process as none of the big cats willingly attacks humans. The first part of the training consisted in overcoming the leopard's instinctive dread of human beings. For this purpose, a leopard born in captivity who had never learned to fear people was far preferable to a wild caught animal. A particularly mean, half-grown cub was selected and a bestiarius, heavily padded, approached the animal deliberately pretending to be nervous. As soon as the leopard made a swipe at him, the bestiarius fell on the cage floor, rolling in apparent agony. The sight of a prostrate victim will generally encourage any aggressive animal to attack and also the man had bits of meat tied to his padding. In this way, the leopard was taught to be a killer. The animal always won in these combats and the trainer was careful never to strike or discipline him in any manner whatever.

The leopard was always fed human meat—there was plenty of that around the arena—and later encouraged to attack slaves. These men had their arms broken and teeth knocked out so they could not injure the animal. A desperate man can kill a leopard with his bare hands (Carl Akeley, the African explorer, accomplished this feat) but even if women or children were used the animal had to be convinced that he could always win without trouble. Finally, when the animal was completely confident of his powers, he was given uncrippled slaves to kill. If the slave put up too much of a struggle, the watching bestiarius helped the leopard out by a quick spear thrust.

Carpophorus' man-eater was a perfectly trained animal. He had developed such a perfect "habit pattern" that he never thought of attacking Carpophorus or anyone except a person exposed on the sand of the training arena. He was used to eating only under these specific conditions and would have starved to death in a butcher shop because he wouldn't have recognized the meat as edible. (This may seem incredible but it's true. A confirmed man-eating lion or tiger will charge through a herd of sheep to get at the shepherd and will not touch a freshly killed cow because he has lost his taste for anything but human flesh. This was true of the famous man-eaters of Tsavo in Kenya, East Africa, who held up the construction of a railroad for three weeks. These two lions ignored goats, cattle and even zebra— the lions' favorite food—left out for them. They finally had to be lured into a double-compartmented trap with two men in one of the compartments. Even with a fusillade of bullets whining about them, they continued to try to reach the men.)

Carpophorus' leopard had become so fixed in this "habit pattern" that the young bestiarius could take him for walks past the antelope herds in the big stockyards where animals intended for the arena were kept. The leopard paid no attention to the antelopes. However, for safety's sake Carpophorus always took him on a leash until one evening when Carpophorus had a little too much wine and he didn't bother to leash the leopard while taking the animal down to drink. By bad luck, something panicked the antelopes and they rushed past the leopard. The sight of the fleeing animals so close to him awoke the big cat's hunting instinct and he sprang on an oryx. Carpophorus tried to drag him off but the leopard clung to the terrified antelope, hanging to the oryx's flank with his long dewclaws. In a blind fury. Carpophorus brought his flail with the lead balls down on the leopard's head and killed him with a single blow.

The young man had killed an animal far more valuable than himself and the raging instructor of the school, to whom Carpophorus had pledged himself as a slave, ordered him thrown to the wild beasts at the next show. Carpophorus accepted his fate in grim silence. But the beasts to be used as executioners were all animals from the stockyards and Carpophorus knew them well. When he was driven into the arena by the circus slaves. Carpophorus strode up to the mixed group of lions, tigers, leopards and bears shouting, "You, Cheops! You, Lesbia! Down, Herod! Good girl, Cypros!" The puzzled animals slunk away and started fighting among themselves. This exhibition so impressed the crowd that they demanded Carpophorus' release and he was sent back to the school. After that, he never again touched wine when working with an animal and made a serious attempt to control his temper.

When Carpophorus graduated from the school, he became a working bestiarius in the arena. Unlike most of his fellows. Carpophorus never lost sight of the fact that his basic job was to please the crowd, not perform some remarkable feat that could only be appreciated by other bestiarii or a few of the connoisseurs on the podium. Having grown up "under the stands" he knew that it was the mob who ran the circus, not the highbrows in the front seats and far less was it the old-time bestiarii who used to meet in the evenings at Chilo's wine shop off the Via Appia and talk of their past triumphs while the respectful younger men sat around and listened. For example, these old-timers considered it a great feat to train stags to pull a chariot. Stags are very nervous animals and only a few bestiarii had ever managed to accomplish this stunt; in Egypt, the animal trainers of Ptolemy had trained stags to pull their royal master, and in Greece, a priestess had appeared in a coach drawn by these dramatic beasts. It was every bestiarius' ambition to duplicate this feat—everyone except Carpophorus. He knew that the public cared nothing about such a stunt, difficult though it might be. They'd just as soon see a chariot drawn by zebras or ostriches which was comparatively easy to do. As a matter of fact, they weren't particularly interested in seeing a chariot drawn by any sort of freak animal. They wanted stronger fare. Carpophorus determined to give it to them.

Sexual relations between a woman and an animal were often exhibited "under the stands" as they are today in the Place Pigalle in Paris. Such exhibitions were occasionally staged in the arena but the trouble was in finding an animal that would perform on schedule. A jackass or even a large dog that would voluntarily mount a woman before a screaming mob was a rare animal and, of course, the woman had to cooperate. The fact that the woman was willing destroyed most of the crowd's fun. Bestiarii had worked hard trying to train animals to rape women, usually covering the woman with the hide of an animal or even building wooden mockups of a cow or a lioness and putting the woman inside. In a play called "The Minotaur," Nero had had an actor playing the part of Pasiphae put in a wooden cow while another actor, dressed as a bull, mounted him. These devices had nearly always failed with real animals and so the whole project had been abandoned.

Carpophorus, with his early training "under the stands" and his practical knowledge of wild animals, understood clearly enough what was the matter. Animals are controlled almost altogether by odor, not by sight. The young bestiarius kept careful watch on all the female animals in the stockyard and when they came into season, collected their blood on soft cloths. These cloths he numbered and put away. Then he got a woman from "under the stands" to help him. Working with extremely tame male animals who didn't mind noise and confusion, he wrapped the woman in the cloths and induced the animals to mount her. As with the man-eaters, he established a habit pattern with these animals, never allowing them to come into contact with a female of their own kind. As the animals grew more confident, they also grew more aggressive. If the woman, following Carpophorus' orders, struggled, a cheetah would sink his dewclaws into her shoulders and grabbing her by the neck with his jaws, shake her into submission. Carpophorus used up several women before he got the animals properly trained— with a bull or a giraffe the woman usually didn't survive the ordeal—but he was always able to get more broken-down old bags from the provinces who didn't fully realize what their job involved until too late.

Carpophorus produced a sensation with his new technique. No one had ever dreamed of having lions, leopards, wild boars and zebra rape women. The Romans were especially fond of acting out mythological scenes in the shows and as Zeus, the king of the gods, often raped young girls in the form of various animals, these scenes could be reenacted in the arena. Under Carpophorus' direction, a bull raped a young girl representing Europa to great applause.

Apuleius has left us an animated account of one of these scenes. A woman who had poisoned five people in order to get their property was sentenced to be thrown to the wild beasts in the arena but first, as an additional punishment and disgrace, she was to be raped by a jackass. A bed was set up in the middle of the arena, inlaid with tortoise shell and provided with a feather mattress and an embroidered Chinese bedspread. The woman was tied spread-eagle on the bed. The jackass had been trained to kneel on the bed, otherwise the business could not have been concluded successfully. When the show was over, wild beasts were turned loose in the arena and quickly put an end to the wretched woman's suffering.

Carpophorus kept his method for training the animals a profound secret, pretending it was all due to a special amulet which he invariably hung around the animal's neck before letting it go into the arena. Although he was offered fabulous prices for this amulet, he refused to sell it. At last, he gave it to his master at the school in return for cancelling his remaining years as a slave. Somehow, the amulet never worked for his master.

The old-time bestiarii were very contemptuous of Carpophorus. They claimed that he had degraded his noble profession by putting on filthy exhibitions. They forgot that in their day they had been criticized by the still earlier bestiarii for training man-eaters to devour helpless men and women. Actually, both groups were right. The shows were growing progressively more and more corrupt. What once had been real exhibitions of courage and skill, even though brutal, were gradually becoming merely excuses for cruelty and perverted sexual exhibitions.

Although Carpophorus boasted that he didn't give a hoot for what the old-timers said, their contempt bothered him. So he continued to fight in the arena as a Venator, once killing twenty wild beasts in one day, presumably with his bare hands. What the beasts were, the accounts don't say. At this savage and dangerous work. Carpophorus was unequaled. As a result, he was the only bestiarius whose name has come down to us.

VI

Borrowing heavily from Martial, Suetonius and other Roman writers, let's picture a day at the Colosseum at the time of the Emperor Domitian during the heyday of the games when Carpophorus was top bestiarius.

For weeks before the show, tickets have been distributed by ward-heelers, thrown to the crowds by the editor giving the games, and sold by speculators. People not fortunate enough to get a ticket have started to line up before the various entrances to the great building days in advance hoping to find standing room. They have brought their food with them and are amused by tumblers, musicians and dancers who hope that the crowd will toss them a few copper coins. The ticket holders are shown to their seats by ushers called locarii: that is, men who show you the right location. Then the soldiers guarding the entrances step aside and there is a frenzied dash for seats in the aisles and standing room in the top tier. It's every man for himself. Women are knocked aside, children trampled, and fights break out in the tangle of passage-ways and ramps leading to the packed tiers. In one such rush, forty people were killed. At last the gigantic building is filled, people crowding so close around the masts holding the awning that the sailors have hard work to handle the rigging.

The whole amphitheater is diffused by a red glow from the light shining through the awning covering the stadium. With this awning for protection, the signs advertising the games need no longer read: "Weather permitting" or "Will go on rain or shine" as they formerly did.

Perfumed fountains shoot colored water into the air, cooling the vast circus and sweetening the atmosphere. Marble statues of various gods and goddesses clasp urns, dolphins and so on from which scented water gushes. The statues could also apparently be made to "sweat" perfumes by some mechanism. The atmosphere takes some sweetening as already it stinks of sweat, leather, garlic and the odor of beasts in the pens below the arena. Later, it will smell a great deal worse.

The moat is filled with water constantly circulating and cooled with snows brought down from the mountains, for by noon the stadium will be like a roasting oven. Summers in Rome are hot and this is one of the summer shows. Without the awning to protect the crowd from the sun, it would be torture to sit in the stadium. Caligula, to punish the mob for criticizing one of his shows, had the awning removed and kept the people in the stadium under the direct rays of the sun for several hours. Many people died of sunstroke. Most of the crowd have brought fans and are wearing their lightest togas or simply sleeveless tunics.

Hawkers selling programs, cool drinks, sweetmeats and cushions to cover the hard marble seats, force their way through the packed aisles as best they can. From the cages below the arena come the roars of lions, the howling of wolves and the trumpeting of elephants. People are busy making bets with each other or with the bookies who crawl from one seat level to another, shouting the current odds on the gladiators. The sound of the crowd is like the noise of "surf in a storm," wrote a Roman poet.

As the awning flaps in the wind, the colors in the stadium change constantly. The awning is made of wool—canvas proved too heavy for the great span—and although it was dyed red over most of its length, there were apparently other colors too, for the Latin poets describe how the waves of light from the swaying awning would tint the white marble of the statues now red, now yellow and now cerulean.

The amphitheater is so high that it makes your head swim to look down from the upper tiers. The wooden planks of the arena are covered with freshly laid, pure white sand especially imported from Egypt for the purpose and sparkles in the subdued light, for semi-precious stones have been sprinkled on it. Nero actually had the arena floor covered with gold dust. This, however, was simply an extravagant gesture. Sand is the best material as it absorbs blood easily—in fact, the word arena means "sand." Around a marble altar in the middle of the arena, priests are conducting a sacrifice. The altar is to Jupiter Latista to whom in the old days human sacrifices were offered. The priests are dressed in white robes with red scarves. They lead out a white bull and two rams wearing gold headdresses. A fire is already burning on the altar and other priests are sprinkling wine and incense on it. After the animals have been sacrificed with much ceremony, the priests examine their entrails to see if the gods wish the games to proceed. With the stadium packed to the bursting point, the gods had better wish it and the pattern of entrails shows that they do. The priests file out, swinging incense burners and chanting hymns, while slaves remove the altar and the carcasses of the animals.

There is a distinguished audience in the podium and the first thirty-six rows of seats reserved for the upper classes. The emperor has not yet arrived, but visiting rulers with their courts are already seated. Blond, bearded Gauls sit staring at the wonders around them. There are Sygambrians with their long tresses tied in knots and Ethiopians with their woolly hair. There are Persians in red, blue and cloth-of-gold gowns, Britons in sleeved coats and loose trousers, Scythians from the Russian steppes, and Greeks in white robes. All these peoples are subject to Rome and the crowd knows it. They make rude comments about the barbarians and even ruder about the lords and ladies in the lower tiers. Many of the patricians have led scandalous private lives which are well-known to the mob. They shout, "Hey, Italicus, are you still your mother's bed-companion?" "Ah, there, Antonia, if the gladiators survive this fight, they'll have a harder time satisfying you." "Greeting, Gaius, have you managed to make your boy friend in the Praetorian Guard a tribune as yet?" The patricians pay no attention to the cries although the taunts sting them. It is beneath their dignity to retort.

From outside the stadium comes the sound of music and a cheer goes up. The procession is coming. Led by slaves in golden armor blowing long trumpets, it files through the Gate of Life. The editor giving the games is riding in a chariot drawn by zebras (the Romans call them "tiger horses") in magnificent harness. He is a sickly young man with a weak face, the son of an influential old patrician woman who is determined to have the inane youngster elected to public office. He looks exhausted already from the long ride through the streets while standing erect in the chariot. The weight of the heavy golden wreath studded with precious stones in his head makes him reel, and a slave has to ride in the chariot with him to hold the wreath in place. The young man is wearing a purple toga covered with gold braid and trying to manage the reins of his chariot and hold up his ivory scepter with its golden eagle at the same time. Luckily for him the reins are simply for show; the zebras are being led by experienced trainers. The crowd gives him an ironic cheer. If the games come up to expectations, they'll give him a real cheer and elect him to office.

A group of musicians march before the chariot playing for all they're worth on horns, fifes and flutes. There is also the usual group of clients surrounding the chariot in their white robes as well as slaves holding up placards saying for what office the young noble is running. After the chariot comes a long series of floats drawn by horses, mules and elephants. On each float is a statue of a god or goddess with priests burning incense on an altar before the image, or a group of young men and girls, posing to represent some mythological tableau. This procession circles the arena to cheers, catcalls, and cries of: "Get down from that chariot and let your mother ride!" and "Oh, I think you're cute, sugar plum. Meet me under the stands and you'll get my vote." These long, formal parades were regarded as a waste of time by the mob and there was even a proverbial expression: "Tiresome as a circensian procession." But, like TV commercials, they were necessary; the editor giving the show wanted people to remember for whom to vote.

The insipid young man descends from the chariot, staggering with weariness, and is half led by his slaves to his place in the podium where his mother is already seated. He collapses with a sigh. Slaves remove his gold wreath and he tries to wipe the sweat off his face with the sleeve of his gown. His mother stops him with an angry gesture.

A trumpet sounds, announcing the entrance of the Emperor Domitian. He enters his box from the rear. The royal box was raised above the podium on a dais. Four columns, each surmounted by a statue of victory, supported a canopy over it. Domitian was a great enthusiast for the games as long as they were cruel enough. (When there were no games, he used to amuse himself sticking pins in flies.) He is a potbellied man with large, watery eyes and completely bald. His private life was such that he was popularly referred to as "the old goat." During the games, he always kept a little boy with an extremely small head by his side and discussed the various events with him, apparently thinking that the deformed child possessed some supernatural ability to pick the winning chariot or best gladiator. Domitian maintained his own school of gladiators and was finally murdered by one of them, hired for that purpose by a group of ambitious politicians.

Domitian doesn't get much of a hand. He isn't giving the games and is unpopular anyway, being regarded as something of a tightwad. The Vestal Virgins enter in their white robes and seat themselves in their box next to the emperor's. Then to another trumpet blast comes the parade of the combatants; the charioteers in their chariots, the gladiators marching in rank after rank, elephants carrying howdahs full of armed men, Nubians on horseback, cavalry from the royal household troop, trained lions led on chains by bestiarii, ostriches drawing light chariots, snake charmers with pythons wrapped around them, male and female bullfighters naked except for loincloths, men in elaborate costumes riding giraffes, stags, antelopes and even a tame rhinoceros, cages drawn by horses containing some of the rarer animals recently brought to Rome, and a group of pygmies from the Ituri Forest in Central Africa.

There are also Parthian bowmen. Syrian slingers, redheaded Irishmen carrying shillelahs, Assyrians with flails, Egyptians with boomerang hatchets, African stone-throwers, Essedarii who use lassos from chariots, Germans with javelins, Sikhs from India with sharp throwing rings, Laplanders with spears and spear-throwers, and inhabitants of the Andaman Islands with harpoons. Little boys dressed as cupids with toy bows and arrows run about shooting light shafts into the crowd, each with a lottery ticket attached to the head. Groups of pretty young girls, nude except for garlands of flowers around their waists, scatter rose petals under the feet of the procession, and dwarfs dressed in extravagant costumes, many with huge, brightly colored phalli strapped to their loins, run about, tumbling, doing handstands, and performing simple acrobatic tricks. A detachment of the Praetorian Guard, their gold armor gleaming in the subdued light, brings up the rear of the procession.

After circling the arena to wild applause, the procession formed before the royal podium and saluted Domitian. They then saluted the young editor who was caught off guard and had to be angrily prompted by his mother before he remembered to rise and make the proper response. Most of the performers left the arena but the gladiators lingered, swaggering around before the crowd and shouting to pretty girls. "Here's your chance, sweetheart, embrace me before death does." Some of the gladiators who were proud of their figures were completely naked except for garlands of flowers on their heads; their bodies shining with olive oil. Instead of weapons, they carried palm branches. These men flexed their muscles, hooking the fingers of one hand under the fingers of the other and straining to make their biceps stand out or, raising both arms at their sides, threw back their shoulders. The crowd shouted and screamed with delight, most of the women looking down coyly but managing to steal a glance out of the corners of their eyes at the magnificent figures before them. Shouts of: "My money's on you, Primus!" "Give 'em the cold steel, Pamphilus!" went up, and there was a desperate last-minute checking of names, odds, and weapons on the programs.

When the arena was cleared, there came a moment's hush. Then the trumpet sounded and immediately hundreds of wild animals began to pour into the arena. This was the usual opening for the games—a venation or wild beast hunt.

The numbers and variety of animals in one of these hunts were astonishing. Martial says that there were nine thousand animals killed in these six-day games. There were deer, wild boars, bears, bulls, antelopes, ibex, jackals, ostriches, cranes, wild horses, hyenas, leopards and a herd of domestic cattle put in for "padding." The whole arena seemed covered with a patchwork quilt of various colored skins. Fights were constantly breaking out but the arena was so crowded and the animals so terrified that by mere weight of numbers the contestants were jostled apart and swept away from each other as the frantic creatures tried to find some way to escape.

The delighted crowd, shouting and counting eagerly on their fingers how many animals there were (for each show had to be bigger than the last), never gave a thought to the enormous labor and astonishing efficiency that made it possible to deliver all these different animals into the arena at the same instant.

When the crowd's interest in the swarming, fighting animals began to lag, foxes with firebrands tied to their tails were set loose. The foxes darted through the packed mass, causing terror wherever they went, while the mob screamed with delight. Domitian, his sluggish nature titivated by the sight of the struggling, helpless beasts, shouted for his bow. The fat emperor was an excellent shot and used to practice his marksmanship on captive animals on his Alban estate. He was handed a powerful sinew-backed bow from Persia, so flexible that when the bow was unstrung, the curve of the bow was the reverse of that taken up when the string was attached. A slave strung the bow while the pudgy ruler danced with impatience and another slave held out a quiver filled with arrows feathered with peacock trains. Domitian began to shoot into the packed animals while the crowd cheered him on. Often he was able to send one arrow through an animal and hit another on the other side. To exhibit his skill, he would shoot two arrows into an animal's head so they resembled horns. After shooting over a hundred of the animals, he ordered a slave to jump into the arena, run to the middle, and hold out his hand with the fingers spread. Domitian sent arrows between the fingers while the crowd yelled with delighted surprise and the patricians politely applauded. As the arena was still full of frantic animals, the slave had quite a job avoiding their wild rushes, and between watching out for the animals and keeping an eye on Domitian, he had a lively time. The crowd thought the slave's antics were excruciatingly funny and laughed until they cried. Suddenly a bull charged the man from behind and tossed him. The slave came down between two bears who instantly seized him and began pulling their victim apart. His cries sounded above the lowing of the cattle and the screams of the wild horses who were kicking on the sand with arrows sticking in them.

Domitian waited with an arrow on the string and a broad smile on his face until the slave was dead. Then with two expert shots, he killed both of the bears and sat down wiping his plump face to thunderous applause.

Now was the turn of the professional venatores, among them Carpophorus. These men entered the arena from the same openings that had emitted the animals. Each group of venators could be instantly identified by the crowd from their equipment. Some men carried only a veil and a long dagger for the bears. Others were in full armor, like gladiators, to receive the charge of the bulls. Others carried spears with a round metal disk halfway up the haft. These would fight the wild boars, the disk being to prevent the boar forcing himself along the spear and killing the man. Other men were on horseback with spears to dispatch the deer. Carpophorus wore only a loose smock that left his powerful arms bare and a few amulets hung around his neck for good luck.

At a signal from the young editor, the trumpet sounded, and while the band played wildly, the venatores rushed into the pass. The next instant the arena was full of screams, brays, howls, bellows, curses, and the noise of the conflict. The crowd loved this spectacle. Being high up and their view of the arena largely obscured by the central ring of masts supporting the awning, they had difficulty watching the individual gladiatorial contests which the nobility in the front row especially enjoyed, but in these venationes there was so much doing that no matter where you sat you could see plenty of action. Everyone was on his feet, shouting encouragement to the venatores although the tumult in the arena was so great that no one could hear his own voice.

Carpophorus worked fast. Leaping from antelope to antelope, he grabbed the wretched creature by the horns, gave the neck one expert twist, and dropping the dying animal seized another. He killed five antelopes in rapid succession . . . then fifteen . . . then twenty. He killed at least one leopard so Martial says. As each animal dropped, there was a bellow of applause from the stands—and not only from the upper tiers, for the patricians were watching Carpophorus also. The shouts came in a regular rhythm like surf as Carpophorus killed animal after animal. Such a feat of strength had seldom been seen in the arena. Carpophorus, according to Martial, was definitely the star of the show.

By now the crowd of animals was thinning out and it was hard for Carpophorus to catch his victims. He adopted a new technique. Putting his hands behind him, he went after the exhausted foxes and frightened jackals that were crouching against the barricade, too terrified to move. Using his teeth alone, Carpophorus caught them by the back of the neck, gave one quick shake, and killed them. Sometimes the animals would turn on the man and sink their teeth into the venator's chin or cheeks. Carpophorus refused to use his hands to pull them off. He shook the animal loose or dislodged it by rolling on the sand and then returned to the attack. The crowd was hysterical by now, Domitian sat with his mouth open and his eyes bulging with delight and even the young editor, sweating and miserable in his heavy toga, took an interest in the proceedings.

The first lot of animals was almost gone and slaves with shovels, baskets, and rakes were hurriedly cleaning the arena. The gratings in front of the chutes began to creak and then slide upwards. Carpophorus shouted a warning to his fellow venatores and took up a position with his back to the inner barrier.

New animals were being driven into the arena and the air was heavy with the odor of burning straw and the stench of singed hair as the slaves used hot irons to force some reluctant beast to move. These new arrivals were not deer, foxes or antelope. They were lions, a few tigers, many leopards, wild dogs and wolves. Without daring to take his eyes from the arena. Carpophorus raised his hands toward the top of the barrier. Instantly his personal slaves handed him a shield and short sword. The slaves of the other venatores also handed their masters new weapons: capes like those used by a modern bullfighter, pikes, javelins, and daggers.

It was not to be expected that these animals would attack the men of their own free will. Freshly captured, bewildered, cramped from long confinement, their only idea was to escape. But there was nowhere for them to go. When they tried to seek refuge along the barrier, slaves with red-hot irons drove them away. Carpophorus selected a young male lion near him and moved forward, covering himself with his shield.

The lion paid no attention to the advancing man. He had got into a snarling argument with another lion. Carpophorus reached his side and then, shortening his sword, struck for the shoulder. At the last instant the lion leaped back to avoid a blow from the other lion and the sword thrust went through the loose skin on his back. The wounded animal spun around and struck at Carpophorus with his forepaws—left, right, like a boxer. Carpophorus took the blows on his shield and the lion backed away, snarling and looking around for some way of escape.

Carpophorus came on. The lion had his back to the barricade now and Carpophorus shouted to the slaves to let him stay there. If the lion was burned suddenly he would make a wild dash across the arena and be impossible to stop. The lion was no longer snarling and was watching the Venator intently. Carpophorus shouted and waves his shield, trying to provoke a charge but the lion would not move. Carpophorus moved back and forth before the animal but the lion still refused to charge. The Venator did not dare to engage the animal against the barrier as he would have no room to dodge. At last, exasperated, he shouted to the slaves, "All right, give him the fire!"

He saw a quick motion through the slit in the barrier. Then the lion gave a roar of pain and shot forward. Carpophorus braced himself, swaying slightly backward to give his forward thrust more power but the desperate animal jumped straight over his head and vanished into the mass of animals.

Carpophorus cursed and turned to find another victim. He saw a leopard crouching on the sand and approached him. The leopard watched him with unblinking eyes and then the venator saw the big cat gather himself together for the spring. Carpophorus hated leopards; they were much too quick. A lion was far easier to handle but this leopard had been the animal nearest to him and he didn't want the crowd to see him avoid it.

He watched carefully from the side of his shield waiting for that lightning-like charge.

As always with leopards, no matter how cautious he was, the charge caught him unexpectedly. One moment the cat had been crouching on the sand. The next instant it was on his shield biting at the boss and trying to get a hold on the smooth bronze with its hind legs. Fortunately an animal could not distinguish between a man and his shield and would continue attacking the shield for some seconds without trying to reach the man. Carpophorus plunged his sword into the leopard's body three times before the mortally wounded cat fell back on the sand, kicking in its death throes.

Carpophorus swung around to find his next quarry. Near him, one of the other venatores had succeeded in blinding a lion by throwing a cape over his head and was giving him the death stroke. Another man had a wolf pinned to the sand with his pike and was leaning on the haft to press the spearhead home, avoiding the snapping jaws to the dying animal. Two of the armored venatores were slowly approaching a tiger from opposite sides, the tiger whirling around in an effort to watch both men at the same time.

A young venator, wild with excitement, flung his javelin and pierced the tiger through the body. Under the circumstances, it was an utterly foolhardy thing to do and Carpophorus, even while the javelin was in the air, knew what would happen. He sprang forward but before he could reach the combatants, the tiger had given a great bound and landed on one of the two armed venatores. The great cat weighed over five hundred pounds and the man went down as though hit by a poleaxe. Instantly the tiger grabbed the man's head in his jaws and crunched the skull, the venator's bronze helmet cracking like tin as the long fangs went through it.

"Spearmen! Spearmen!" shouted Carpophorus at the top of his lungs while trying to distract the tiger's attention. A venator armed with a spear run up and tried to drive it through the tiger's shoulder but the cat sprang back, striking at the spearhead with his paw. Then he spun around in a circle, biting at the javelin in his body.

Carpophorus shouted to the armed venator, "Take him on the other side while I move in from here!" The venator nodded and circled the tiger. Carpophorus snapped to the spearman, "All right, we'll keep him busy until you get a chance to use your spear but don't take all day about it." Settling his shield, he came in toward the tiger.

The tiger had stopped biting at the javelin and was facing Carpophorus. His hindquarters were slightly raised so he could bring his rear legs under him and get the maximum spring for his bound. Carpophorus moved slightly to the right to give the spearman a better chance. The tiger's eyes followed him but the cat did not change its position.

Then, without any more intimation than the leopard had shown, the tiger charged. Carpophorus dropped to one knee to receive the shock, covering himself with his big shield. The tiger hit the shield like a battering ram, knocking it out of the man's hand. Then he grabbed Carpophorus' right shoulder with his teeth and started to drag him across the arena.

Carpophorus stabbed upwards into the tiger's belly. As he did so, he saw the spearman's blade flash past him and plunge deep into the tiger's chest. The armed Venator came in and with one terrible stroke split the tiger's skull open with his sword. The dead animal fell across Carpophorus.

The other venatores pulled him from under the striped carcass. Carpophorus was streaming blood but could still stand. Around them other fights were raging. A venator had a leopard by the throat and was trying to strangle it although the cat's slashing hind legs had already disemboweled him. Four wild dogs, huge, yellow Molossians from the mountains of Greece, had got another venator down and were stretching him out on the sand, two pulling him by the face and shoulder and two holding him by the legs. A fifth dog rushed in and attacked the helpless man's genitals. Another Venator was trying to get his pike out of a wolf's body while being attacked by other members of the pack. A young venator had grabbed a lioness by the tail and was holding her while two of his companions stabbed the animal with their pikes.

"You'd better leave the arena," said the armed venator to Carpophorus. "The crowd will let you go." The crowd had been watching Carpophorus' feat and were giving him a big hand.

Carpophorus hardly heard him. He was blind with rage and had a sudden savage hatred of the beasts. He stooped and tried to pick up his sword but his side was numb where the tiger had been shaking him. He cursed and the spearman picked up the sword for him. By an effort, Carpophorus made his fingers close over the hilt although he could feel nothing.

He started forward toward the melee, blood from his wounded side filling up the footprints made by his right foot as he staggered on. The armed venator and the spearman exchanged looks, shook their heads, and followed him. The crowd were shouting, "No, Carpophorus, no!" and waving their handkerchiefs but Carpophorus paid no attention to them. He was going to get himself another tiger or die trying.

Domitian turned and gave an order to a courtier behind him. The man shouted to the trumpeter who gave a single blast on his long horn. From the Gate of Life marched a detachment of heavily armed soldiers armed with spears. These men formed a line across the far end of the arena and then locked their shields together, each shield fitting into a bracket on the shield next to it until there was a solid shield wall stretching across the arena. The great rectangular shield covered a man from the bridge of his nose to his knees. Before the shields was a solid line of spears held in such perfect alignment that from the side it seemed as though there were only one weapon. At an order from the centurian in command, the line moved forward at the regulation legion step, so perfectly timed that it could be used, to measure distances. A thousand (milla) such steps measured exactly 5,280 feet, or what has later become known as a mile.

Behind the line of troops came bestiarii with their lead-tipped cat-o'-nine-tails in case any of the beasts broke through the soldiers. Behind them came gladiators called andabatae, men wearing helmets without a visor so they could not see. As soon as they reached the arena, these andabatae began to swing wildly around trying by chance to hit one another. The andabatae were necessary for the hunt was now over and even while the arena was being cleared, there had to be something going on.

As soon as he heard the trumpet signal the end of the hunt the Master of the Games, who functioned as ringmaster, gave orders to open the doors of the chutes. The order was immediately obeyed and slaves hurriedly put out basins of water to help lure the exhausted animals inside. Before the steadily advancing line of spears, the remaining animals gave back. Most of them eventually found the open doors of the chutes and rushed in, drinking feverishly from the basins. A few charged the soldiers and died under the spears. Two lions and a leopard managed to force their way through the serried ranks; the lions leaping over the men and the leopard fighting his way through. The animals were promptly driven out through the Gate of Life by the bestiarii with their flails.

Carpophorus, still in a daze, did not at first understand what was happening. He continued to stride toward the remaining beasts looking for another tiger. The spearman pulled at the bloody sleeve of his tunic.

"The hunt's over, Carpophorus," he said softly. "The soldiers are clearing the arena for the next act. Come on, let's get out of here."

Carpophorus shrugged him off. A wolf trying to escape from the spears ran past him and Carpophorus kicked at the animal irritably. There were no tigers left.

The crowd had forgotten about the hunt by now and were watching the andabatae, roaring with laughter at the men's clumsy swings. Slaves followed the andabatae, pushing them together with long forked poles. Carpophorus saw a lion and plunged toward the animal. Martial says that rather than face him, the lion rushed on the spears and was killed.

The line of soldiers was almost up to Carpophorus now. The centurion was yelling, "Get that crazy bastard out of here."

A venator with a cape stepped up quietly behind Carpophorus and threw the cape over his head. Instantly the armed venator and the spearman grabbing the raging bestiarius. They dragged him out of the arena while Carpophorus fought like a madman. Under the stands, the arena doctors were waiting.

"All right, boys, bring him in here," said one of the doctors taking command. Carpophorus was pulled into a small room where several of the venatores were under treatment. The doctor shouted and four giant Africans hurried over. Instantly grasping the situation, they seized the raging venator and pulled him to a wooden bed with shackles at the top and bottom. For a gladiator or a venator to go made with wounds or bloodlust—berserk, the Norsemen used to call it—was a common occurrence. Carpophorus struggled with superhuman strength but the Africans were expert manhandlers and he had no chance.

They flung him down on the heavy wooden frame and shackled his arms and legs.

"You'll feel better in a few minutes, my boy," said the doctor soothingly as he prepared a potion containing opium. "Some fight you put up. Those tigers are hell, aren't they? Now some people think that; lions are worse because they roar and put on a big show, but any good venator can handle a lion. Drink this." He grabbed the raving man's cheek, taking care not to be bitten, pulled it away from the gums, and skillfully poured the draft down Carpophorus' throat. "I'll never forget the ludi sollemnes that old Vitellius gave to get the people's minds off the Pannonian mutiny. Fifty tigers in the arena at one time. That was a day! Blood all over the place. Does this man have to fight again today?" he shouted to the Master of the Games who was hurrying past.

"No, but he will tomorrow afternoon," said the Master as he went by.

"You'll be all right by then," the doctor assured Carpophorus, who was now sobbing in great, heaving gasps. "I'll have the slaves squeeze some blood out of those dead cats and you can drink that. You've lost plenty of blood but that will restore it as well as feed your spirit. Now let's sew up that cut in your shoulder."

VII

Outside in the arena while the andabatae were slugging it out, slaves were busy rolling out a model of a mountain through the Gate of Death up to the inner barrier. On it were live trees, flowers, flowering shrubs, and even streams of running water, kept flowing by pumps worked by slaves in the interior. Set designers scurried over the mountain making last-minute changes and carpenters checked to be sure that everything was in working order.

The Master of the Games was watching anxiously as the wretched andabates slashed each other with wild blows, seldom inflicting a mortal wound. The real gladiators who were known to the mob and had a chance of putting up a good fight might be given the thumbs-up signal but these miserable creatures, always condemned criminals of the lowest order, were unknown and could show no skill. Their only hope was to exhibit such a desperate courage that the mob might be kind enough to have one or two spare for another day. So they fought with the mad bravery of desperation. As a man fell, an arena servant, dressed as Charon who ferried souls across the River Styx, motioned to slaves who followed him with a brazier full of hot coals in which irons were constantly being heated. With a hot iron, he tested the man to see if he were still alive. If the fallen man twitched when the hot iron was applied, another arena servant dressed as Hermes, a god of the underworld, motioned his slaves to cut the rawhide straps that kept the andabate's helmet in place. Then he hit the prostate man over the head with a hammer. Instantly the regular arena slaves stuck hooks in the corpse and dragged it out through the Gates of Death to the spoliarium where slaves stripped off the armor. The body was then turned over to butchers who cut it up to feed the wild animals.

Although the patricians in the lower tier of seats regarded the pointless struggles of the andabates with contempt, the crowd loved them. They pretended to shout advice to the fighters, yelling, "He's on your left! No, now he's on your right!" deliberately fooling the blindfolded men to see them whirl around in terror and frantically slice the air. But with the help of the slaves using the long forked poles, the remaining andabates were pushed together and the end was near. The Master of the Games turned to shout to the crews on the mountain: "Get off it or, by the gods, I'll leave you up there! All right, slaves, strike the set!"

At the beginning of the andabates' fight, slaves had taken their positions behind the inner barricade. A slave with a long pole Was standing by each of the elephant tusks supporting the overhand net. Others stood ready with their hands on the planks running between the masts which supported the awning. At the Master of the Games' cry, the slaves with the poles lifted the net off hooks set in the tusks so the whole net came to the ground, like a great tennis net a hundred yards long. At the same time, the other slaves were slipping the planks out of their brackets on the sides of the masts. As the planks came loose, still other slaves seized them and rushed them out of the arena. As the last planks were removed, the net was grabbed and pulled back between the masts to be hurried after the planks. The spectators now had a much better view of the arena although the central ring of masts still remained.

Meanwhile, the construction and planning crews on the artificial mountain leaped to the group while gangs of slaves, possibly assisted by trained elephants pushing with their fore-heads, moved the great mass forward on rollers. There were two empty spaces in the central ring of masts holding the overhead awning; one in front of the Gate of Life (over which was the imperial podium) and the other before the Gate of Death . . . the sag in the awning being supported by overhead guy ropes at these points. The mountain was rolled into the arena from the Gate of Death through one of these gaps.

The fight between the andabates was now just about over. Only two couples were left. These men had thrown away their shields, joined their left hands so as not to be parted, and were stabbing at each other with their swords. In one couple, the men killed each other. The arena slaves were rapidly and efficiently clearing out the remaining corpses and spreading fresh sand on the arena floor. At last, one of the two remaining andabates killed the other. A shout of "Peractum est!" went up and the surviving andabate was led from the arena. Now he had at least a few days' respite until another exhibition of andabates was forthcoming.

As the slaves raced from the arena carrying the last of the corpses, pipes set in the podium wall were turned on and began to flood the arena. The Master of the Games appeared on the podium and shouted that he had an important announcement to make. Actually, this announcement should have been made by the young editor but he had been drinking huge quantities of cold wine and could hardly stand, let alone address the crowd. The Master of the Games shouted:

"Romans, it has been said that we are not a cultural people. Nothing could be farther from the truth. Simply because we are a strong, virile race and enjoy manly sports does not mean that we don't appreciate the finer things in life." He was interrupted by boos, catcalls, and unpleasant noises made by placing the tongue between the lips and blowing hard. Someone threw a wine skin which he dodged. "Yes, looking at your noble, intelligent faces, my friends, I know that the next act will deeply appeal to the artistic nature for which Romans are famous. We have with us today the distinguished Greek singer, Mezentius, who will sing that beautiful ode 'The Death of Orpheus' while accompanying himself on the lyre. As you know, Orpheus was the famous musician in Greek legend who could charm even wild animals with his music. Ladies and gentlemen, I give you the great Mezentius!"

Amid bellows of indignant rage from the crowd, an artificial rock on the summit of the mountain swung open and out stepped Mezentius, draped in a white gown and carrying a golden lyre. While the furious crowd screamed: "We've been swindled! Back to Athens, you damn fruit! What is this, the games or a musical? Wreck the joint!" the musician bowed to right and left and then struck the opening chords of the song. There were now a couple of feet of water in the arena and the Master of the Games, who had been anxiously watching the plumb marks on the podium wall, gave a signal. A flat-bottomed barge covered with beautiful girls and hung with garlands of flowers floated out, the girls singing an accompaniment to the song. As the girls were naked except for tiny gauze aprons which the motion of the barge kept blowing aside or pressing against their plump young thighs, the crowd stopped booing and began to take an interest in the proceedings. Now that he could be heard, the musician redoubled his efforts and the girls sang for all they were worth, waving their arms in time to the music and keeping their shoulders well back so that their breasts with the nipples carefully rouged would stand out. Meanwhile, a new novelty was introduced. From crates and cages, slaves were slipping crocodiles and six hippopotami into the rapidly rising waters. The crowd began to applaud.

The barge, moved by paddlers hidden in the interior, drifted closer to the mountain where Orpheus sat among the flowers pouring out the words of the immortal ode. The water in the arena was so clear that the crowd could watch the animals swimming in it, the great crocodiles, fifteen feet long, gliding along like shadows and the ponderous hippos walking on the bottom as though on land. Occasionally one of the hippos would rise to the surface, blow two columns of spray into the air, and then sink again. The crowd watched with interest for a few minutes and then began to grow restless.

The Master of the Games was an expert in timing. He sensed to the second when the crowd had had enough. He gave another signal.

Instantly a series of hidden doors on the sides of the mountain slid open and out wandered a number of wild beasts: leopards, bears, wolves and black panthers. Orpheus, absorbed in his singing, did not notice the animals until a panther strolled across the grassy turf directly in front of him. The horrified musician stared in astonishment but continued his song, looking around him desperately and trying to signal the Master of the Games that a horrible mistake had been made. The girls continued singing gaily, tossing rose petals toward Orpheus and urging him to let them hear more of his golden voice.

But the unfortunate singer was no longer interested in educating the Roman mob. He dropped his lyre and began to run wildly around the mountain, screaming for help. The crowd laughed until they were sick. It was well-known that the elegant Greeks considered themselves superior to their Roman conquerors and here was one of the effeminate creatures putting on a typical exhibition of cowardice. Also, this sudden twist had been completely unexpected, which is the basic element in all humor. A man shouted, "All right, you Greeks think you're so damn cultured, let's see you soothe these wild beasts with your high-toned music!" and the crowd went into another roar of laughter.

The unhappy Orpheus dashed around a rock and ran head on into a leopard. The frightened animal sprang back and then struck at the man. His claws caught in the Greek's robe and both man and beast went down together, the leopard mad with terror trying to disengage himself. At the sight of struggling figures, two wolves rushed in and began to maul the man. Now one of the bears, a trained man-eater, saw the fight and began to shuffle forward. He stood swaying his long, snakey neck back and forth and then made a sudden rush. He cuffed the nearest wolf away and grabbing the singer by the leg started to drag him off, snuffling and grunting to himself. The leopard, still caught by his claws, was pulled along also. The wolves followed hopefully. Another bear came in from the other side and grabbed the screaming musician by the arm. The two animals pulled the man apart while the wolves rushed in to finish the job. The leopard made another frenzied attempt to free himself and this time succeeded. He dashed up the side of the hill and collided with another bear who was coming down to see what the trouble was. The two animals instantly began to fight while some of the ever-present wolves bounded up to pull down the loser.

The musician was dead and the animals were fighting for the parts of his body strewn over the hillside. The crowd was weak from laughter and the girls on the barge were laughing too. The Master of the Games gave another signal.

This time nothing seemed to happen. Then one of the girls

on the barge suddenly gave a shriek of terror. She was seated on the gunwale and the water in the arena was washing against her bare feet. The barge was sinking. The other girls took fright. Jumping up, they began screaming for help. A slave inside the barge had been watching through a knothole for the Master of the Game's signal. When it came, he gave orders to pull out the plugs and sink the vessel. The paddlers inside the barge had escaped through a hatch and were now feverishly swimming for the podium wall, praying that they could reach it before the crocodiles and hippos got them.

Hippos are by no means the big, good-natured pig-like creatures that they seem. These animals were all bulls and in a very bad temper. A slave happened to touch one of the creatures. Instantly the hippo swung around, making the water swirl around him, and plunged his great tusks into the man's body. As the red dye spread, the crocs began to thrash around, sometimes seizing a hippo, by the leg and sometimes each other. The crowd rose to its feet as one man at this new spectacle. The barge full of screaming girls was now awash and some of the more determined girls had plunged into the water and were trying to swim to the mountain island or reach the podium.

Few of them made it for the Master of the Games had carefully selected girls who were non-swimmers. Those who reached the mountain were promptly attacked by the wild animals, now crazed by the scent of blood and the taste of the dead Greek. A few reached the podium wall and clung to it, screaming for mercy. The water around the barge was churned white as the crocs attacked the girls that still clung to the wreck. Two of the mighty reptiles seized one girl and began twisting in opposite directions. One wrung off a leg, the other an arm. One gigantic animal that must have weighed well over a ton reared out of the water and grabbed a girl standing on the gunwale.

He submerged with her, carrying the shrieking girl as easily as an elephant carrying a carrot. Others of the enormous saurians were trying to knock the girls into the water with their tails. The barge, being made of wood, did not sink completely but there was no protection on it for the women.

Several of the hippos were approaching the barge, excited by the noise and the smell of blood. Although not carnivorous, the big brutes were as aggressive as bulls. Only their eyes and noses showed above the water as they floated studying the hysterical excitement on the remains of the barge. The crowd was furious. People yelled. "Go on there, you big slobs! Do something! Get the fire!" for bulls that would not perform were occasionally goaded into action by throwing burning javelins into them.

Then one of the hippos charged the barge. Lifting his head and shoulders out of the water and opening his huge mouth to its fullest capacity, he plunged his two tusks over the gunwale and began to worry the vessel like a terrier shaking a rat. The submerged wreck heaved and shook as two tons of enraged hippo struggled with it. The last of the screaming girls were flung into the water and the white bellies of the crocs flashed as they twisted in the water, trying to wring off pieces of their prey.

The mob was now uncontrollable. Women stood up in the stands drumming with their fists on the backs of people in the seats before them and screaming hysterically: "Kill! Kill! Kill!" Even before the games started, smart young men could spot women who would give way to this madness and make a point of sitting next to them. While in the grip of hysteria, the women were unconscious of everything else and the boys could play with them while they screamed and writhed at the bloody spectacle below them. Old men, long impotent, sat drooling gleefully. Even ordinarily normal men watched with mouths hanging half open, eyes staring eagerly to take in every detail, and then fought their way out through the crowd to take advantage of the prostitutes assembled in the arches under the building. Children shouted and danced on their seats, as much to relieve their nervous tension as with joy at the sight below them. Only in the lower ring of seats were there connoisseurs who watched with dispassionate interest, commenting to each other on the strength and ferocity of the animals and criticizing the girls' figures as they were dragged to their death.

From above the watertight barrier which had been hastily erected across the Gate of Death, rafts made of reeds and two-man boats of woven rushes were being launched. The rafts held six men each, Africans from the cataracts of the Nile armed with harpoons. In each of the rush boats which had extravagantly high bows and sterns sat a single harpooner and one paddler. These curious craft were paddled toward the seething water around the remnants of the barge. One of the rafts silently glided toward a hippo and, at a given signal, the harpooners all plunged their harpoons into the massive back.

Now even the blasé occupants of the podium became interested. The whole arena was quickly converted into a mass of foam, blood, struggling reptiles, bellowing hippos and shouting men. Several light dugout canoes shot out. All but one headed for the mountain and a number of Egyptians stepped ashore. Bestiarii had already come out of the interior of the structure and were driving the animals back into their holes with the lashing, lead-tipped whips. The Egyptians lined up along the water's edge and stood with folded arms. They were magnificently built men, naked except for loincloths, and they stood motionless as images. They had brought several heavy nets which lay beside them carefully coiled.

In the remaining dugout was a lean, wiry man who from his coloring was probably half Egyptian and half African. His dugout was manned by four expect paddlers who made the light craft fly. He seemed to be directing the harpooning, peering down into the water and then ordering the harpooners to take that animal or spare the next. The crowd shouted furiously at him. "No! No!" but the man ignored them. When the angry cries of the mob rose to such a pitch that it seemed as though a riot threatened, Domitian turned to one of his aides and snapped an order. The aide vanished and returned in a few moments with the Master of the Games. He gave the emperor some explanation that seemed to satisfy him for he nodded and continued to watch the show.

The water level in the arena was dropping rapidly, for sluice gates had been opened and the water was pouring out even more swiftly than it had flowed in. All the hippos were dead now or in their death agonies and many of the crocs had been finished off by the harpooners. The lean man in the dugout had landed on the mountain and was giving orders to the others. They lifted the nets and began to wade into the water which was now not much above their waists. The crowd grew silent, sensing that something unusual was about to take place.

The water was now so clouded by blood that it was impossible to see through it but the men prodded about with long poles. Then they raised a shout. Splashing through the muck, they made a circle with the net and then began to drag it up the slope of the mountain. There was a violent underwater explosion and a great crocodile reared up in the center of the net. The men dragged it ashore and their leader stepped forward. The croc was thrashing about fiercely, striking at the men with his great tail and snapping his jaws together with a report that could be heard in the topmost tier of seats. Watching his chance, the Egyptian made a sudden plunge and, landing on the reptile's back, locked his arms around the saurian's neck.

The most sincere of all applause—a great gasp—went up

from the crowd. Never had they seen anything like this. The croc began to roll and it was all the Egyptian's assistants could do to keep him from going back into the water. One man made the mistake of grabbing the gigantic creature by the tail and was knocked unconscious. Gradually the Egyptian locked his legs around the reptile and then, getting a half nelson on him, slowly turned him over. Then he quickly grabbed the croc by the muzzle, holding his jaws shut. At this incredible feat of strength, the crowd shrieked, with astonishment and delight.

With the crocodile still on its back, the man carefully let go the jaws and then ran one hand down the animal's belly. He stood up, holding his hand palm down toward the reptile and making mystic passes in the air with the other. The huge creature lay motionless while the crowd held its breath. Then the Egyptian turned to take his bow.

He got his applause, full scale, although there were many who touched their amulets and made the sign of the evil eye, muttering. "Black Magic!" When the applause had died down, the Egyptian turned and touched the crocodile with his foot. After a kick or two, the reptile rolled over and turned on the man with open mouth but the men with the net were ready. The saurian was quickly swathed in the meshes and dragged out of the now dry arena while the slaves rushed in with teams of mules to remove the dead hippos and crocodiles.

Carpophorus had managed to persuade the doctor to let him up so he could see the completion of this performance. Shaky from his emotional outburst as well as from loss of blood, he walked slowly to the Gate of Death, putting his hand against the wall occasionally to support himself. *No one paid any attention to him.* The gladiators for the next turn were warming up by swinging their weapons and practicing cuts at each other, blocks and pulleys were being fastened to the artificial mountain preparatory to pulling it from the arena, cages were being brought up to secure the animals still inside the great structure, slaves with wheelbarrows of dry sand were trying to force their way through the mob coming in from the arena, and the Master of the Games was directing the organized chaos. Carpophorus managed to force himself forward, occasionally losing his temper and cuffing a slave who jostled him, until he could see the upper tiers of seats and part of the awning framed in the curve of the gateway. Now that he was almost out of the tunnel, the full force of the crowd's yells reached him. Curiously, while fighting himself, Carpophorus never heard the crowd; he was always too intent on the business at hand. But he knew the high-pitched cries that meant the mob was really being carried out of itself and eagerly pushed his way forward.

He was first conscious of the odor of the damp sand mixed with the stench of the disemboweled animals. The venador was accustomed to the smell of death but this was the first time he smelled it in conjunction with dampness. He saw the Egyptian wrestle the crocodile and was deeply interested, but with his technician's trained eye, he also saw that it was not nearly as dangerous as it seemed to the crowd. Although he had never seen crocodile wrestling, he knew that it had been exhibited in the Roman arena at the time of Augustus—in the Bestiarii School the teacher had read accounts of the feat from Pliny and Strabo. He watched attentively while three more of the Egyptian's team wrestled crocs after they had first been caught in nets, each time to tremendous applause. When the Egyptians finally withdrew and the gladiators marched in, led by a band, Carpophorus made a point of meeting the Egyptian in the dressing room and standing him a cup of cooled wine.

The Egyptian was more affable than Carpophorus had feared

he might be. Generally, a performer didn't care to discuss the technique of his routine; there was too much danger some ambitious rival would steal it. But this man was obviously flattered that a Roman—and although only a freeman, Carpophorus was a Roman—would deign to praise his act. After a couple of mugs of strong wine, the Egyptian relaxed.

"Well, it's a good act, a good act," he said modestly. "I'm from Tentyra—that's on the Nile in southern Egypt—and the traditional business in our village has always been hunting crocs for their skins." Carpophorus nodded. Nearly every small town had some traditional profession and crocodile skins brought a good price as leather. "Some of the young men used to wrestle eight and nine-foot crocs for fun. It's not as dangerous as it looks if you watch out for the tail and jaws. Crocs are pretty sluggish, you know, not like trying to tackle a leopard or a lioness as you do."

"Every man to his own. I'd hate to tackle a twenty-foot croc," said Carpophorus, filling his friend's cup again and already making plans to add crocodile wrestling to his repertoire.

"It takes practice, but with enough leverage you can turn one over on his back just as you would a man. Not one twenty feet long. That would weigh over a ton, and besides they don't come that big often. That one you saw me wrestle was fifteen feet long, and let me tell you, that's plenty of croc!"

"I could have sworn he was bigger," said Carpophorus flatteringly. "What was the magic charm you used to keep him on his back?"

"Oh, that was business for the crowd. They think we Egyptians are full of magic. Any croc will lie still if you turn him over on his back like that. I don't know why it is; they just do."

"But think of the strength it took to hold his mouth closed," Carpophorus exclaimed admiringly.

"Nothing to it. A croc's jaw power comes when he closes his jaws. They've got tremendous power there. But any good men can hold the jaws shut."

"Well, well, you certainly know your business," said Carpophorus. Privately, he was thinking what a fool the man was to give away this information. At the next games, Carpophorus would put on his own exhibition of crocodile wrestling.

"The big problem is getting them tame," the Egyptian went on, holding out his cup for more wine. "Some of the sacred crocs get very tame. The priests can call them out of the water and feed them by hand. If a croc isn't tame, he won't eat in captivity, and also they're too nervous to attack swimming humans unless they see others start doing it."

"We have the same trouble with lions," Carpophorus told him. You have to put a 'make-lion' who's a real man-eater in with a new bunch. Once they see the make-lion start killing, the others will join them."

"I had an idea that was the way you worked it. There's a big tame croc on a great lake in the heart of Africa. He is nearly twenty-five feet long and must weigh as much as an elephant. The natives use him as a combined judge and executioner. A suspected criminal is led to the lake shore and the priests call the croc by beating on drums. The croc knows what the drums mean and comes swimming across the lake and crawls up the bank. Then the victim is pushed toward him with long poles. If the croc eats the man, he's considered guilty. If for some reason the croc won't bother with him, he's set free. That croc's so old and feeble now that a native has to help him climb the bank by carrying his tail like a train. I'd love to get my hands on that animal. What a sensation he'd make in Rome!"

"Just how do you go about getting them tame in the first place?" asked Carpophorus casually, refilling the empty cup.

"That, dear friend, is my little secret," said the Egyptian calmly as he drained the cup and rose. "I've got to see how those four crocs are getting along that we saved. Those are our tame stock; we don't let them get killed. Thanks for the wine. Don't get drunk and start giving away secrets."

Black-bellied bastard, thought Carpophorus to himself as he watched the Egyptian's retreating back. Who does he think wants to steal his lousy act anyhow? That's the trouble with those Egyptians, always suspicious. I hope that damned croc of his eats him next week in Verona.

VIII

It was noon now. The gladiators who had gone out after the crocodile hunt were Meridiani, second string men who fought during the middle of the day when most of the patricians had gone home for lunch and only the mob remained. In the stands, baskets of food were opened, flasks of wine produced, and the mob picnicked while the unfortunates below them fought to the death.

During this slack period, the Master of the Games stopped long enough to speak to Carpophorus. "How are you holding up?" he asked, glancing at the mass of bloody bandages covering the venador's right side.

"I'm all right," said Carpophorus sullenly. As an experienced bestiarius, he hated to think of any animal, even a tiger, getting the best of him.

The Master of the Games considered. "Immediately after the noon period, we're going to have a holocaust of prisoners. They're to be killed by lions but I want to save the good man-eaters until the next day. If the man-eaters are used today, they'll be gorged and won't work in the legendary pageants scheduled for tomorrow. But we don't want any holdups in the show. The new lions will have to attack the prisoners at once; no running around against the barrier or crouching down in the sand."

"What do you expect me to do?" snarled Carpophorus. "Wild lions won't attack people without trained man-eaters in the arena."

"Don't argue with me, just see that it's done," retorted the Master of the games coldly. "Remember that there are five more days of these games ahead of us. Give me any more of your lip and I'll have you in there with another tiger and your hands tied behind you." The Master of the Games strode away.

After grumbling to himself Carpophorus began to think. It was not the Master of the Games' threat that bothered him; it was his own reputation as a bestiarius who could perform miracles. For a long while he sat with his head in his hands, snarling at the slaves dragging the dead Meridiana over his feet but refusing to move from the passageway. Then he had an idea, and rising painfully, headed for the lower pits where the prisoners were kept.

He went down ramp after ramp. Because they were easier to move and also not so valuable, the prisoners condemned to death in the arena were kept in the lowest levels while the animals were in the upper cells. Carpophorus had seldom been down here and had to ask his way constantly of the guards stationed at intervals by the torches burning in brackets on the wall. Finally he reached the level he was seeking and after a long walk and many turns arrived in front of the oaken door where the captives to die that afternoon were kept.

They were Jews, taken prisoner during one of the many spasmodic uprisings in Palestine. Carpophorus vaguely remembered some account of the business. Three villages high in the Masada hills had revolted. Why, he couldn't recall. Either they had objected to the eagles on the legionnaires' standards, calling them graven images, or they had attacked a caravan because it was owned by Sarmatians or some such thing. Anyhow, it had taken a three months' campaign to unearth them from their forts in the cliffs and men, women and children had been sent to die in the arena. The Jews were always a troublesome people but if it wasn't for them the Colosseum might never have been built. After the fall of Jerusalem in 72 A.D., twelve thousand Jewish prisoners had worked on the construction of the great building and later had been killed there in the inauguration ceremonies.

The guards at the door slid back the heavy bolts, eagerly asking him for tips on the regular gladiatorial contests coming up late that afternoon. Carpophorus knew little about the gladiators but he told them to back Negrimus against Priedens, and entered the dark room. At this level, the only air vents led to the floor above instead of to the outside and there was no light except that cast by a single torch in a wall bracket. The people were singing some sort of chant in a foreign language and Carpophorus looked them over. Mostly women, children and old men with long beards. Nearly all the young men must have been killed in the fighting. That suited Carpophorus' plans perfectly.

The crowd paid no attention to him and he had to shout to stop their singing. Finally the hymn ceased and Carpophorus called, "Do any of you speak Latin?"

No one answered so Carpophorus tried again in Greek.

An old man answered in the same tongue. "I speak Greek but in spite of that, I want it clearly understood that I am not a Sadducee nor do I have any sympathy with those of my people who learn other tongues and other ways."

"Sure, sure," said Carpophorus impatiently. "Now I have a proposition to make. We're using a bunch of raw lions and they won't attack unless you do exactly what I tell you to do. Now wait a minute," he went on, holding up his hand. "Even if the lions don't attack, it only means we'll have to use bears or wild dogs and they'll kill you much more slowly than the lions will. Here's my proposition. You have a lot of kids here. Only the kids who are sick or crippled and will die anyhow have to go into the arena with you. I'll use my influence with the Master of the Games to get the rest sold as slaves. I swear it by my gods."

"I am sure that we would all prefer to die together," said the old rabbi with dignity. "Nevertheless, I will repeat your offer."

He repeated it while Carpophorus waited impatiently. The lack of oxygen in the room was making him dizzy and the stink was sickening. There were no toilet facilities and the crowd of victims had been kept there over a week. No wonder, Carpophorus reflected, that prisoners often dashed out into the arena as eagerly as though they were being given their freedom. Any fate was better than being cooped up here, and even a few minutes' chance to get fresh air before the wild beasts attacked was a luxury. He also understood why these holocausts were generally given on the first day of the games. The prisoners had to be got out of these cells as fast as possible before they all died.

When the rabbi had repeated the message, there was a wild outcry from the women. They screamed, clung to their children, and rocked back and forth in an ecstasy of grief. Many of the men sank down and buried their faces in their hands, openly weeping. Carpophorus regarded this exhibition of emotion with disgust; as a Roman, he had been trained to conceal his feelings. He wondered how the old rabbi could make any sense out of the confusion for everyone seemed to be talking to him at once, waving their hands, tearing their rags of clothing and holding out their palms to him as though expecting help. The rabbi listened calmly to the outburst, occasionally asking a question and shaking his head. Finally he turned to Carpophorus.

"I still think it would be far better if we all died together but the women are weak and will accept your offer. What is that you want us to do?"

Carpophorus was ready for that question. The technique he was about to explain was later observed by Eusebius, one of the fathers of the early church, among the Christian martyrs. Exactly the same technique is used today by white hunters in Africa to induce animals to charge for photographic purposes or bring them in range for an easy shot.

"Well, first of all you've got to understand how these animals think," he started briskly. This was his great subject and he felt contemptuous of these ignorant heathen who knew nothing of the mental workings of the great cats. "A lot of people think that starving a lion or a tiger makes 'em vicious. I've seen cats so starved that when they were turned loose in the arena, they lay down and died at the feet of the people they were supposed to eat." Carpophorus shook his head sadly at such bungling. "Starving a cat only makes him weak. You've got to remember that most of the big cats can go for long periods of time without eating and then their stomach juices stop flowing. Even in a quiet cage, it's hard to make them eat under these conditions, so you can imagine what it's like getting them to attack strange prey in an open arena with that mob yelling their heads off."

"Exactly what is it that you wish us to do?" asked the rabbi patiently.

"I'm getting to that," snapped Carpophorus. "If you people just stand still, these raw lions won't pay any attention to you. Keep trying to remember that you don't smell like their natural prey so the poor things don't even know that you're good to eat. We'll try to help out there by covering you with zebra and ante-lope skins so you'll seem more like their ordinary quarry. Now if you shout or yell or start running around, you'll scare them.

Lions are very sensitive creatures. In a wild state, they only hunt at night, there can't be any moon, it's the female who does the actual killing, the weather must be just right and lots of other factors that we can't reproduce here. So don't start yelling or screaming as those women were doing just now or you'll scare the yellow porridge out of these cats."

"The women will be quiet, I promise you," said the rabbi calmly.

"Well, see that they are. Remember you've got nobility sitting in those boxes and just the jewels they're wearing are worth more than the whole lot of you. Nothing personal, you understand, just stating a fact. All right, now here's what you've got to do. Stand quiet and spread out some so you don't form a compact mass. Then move your hands slightly and sway your bodies a little; just enough so the lions know you're alive. Once they realize that you're alive but not dangerous, they'll charge. Remember, no quick motions or loud noises. Easy does it."

"I understand," said the rabbi. He turned and translated. The people listened despairingly. A new volley of questions went up and the rabbi asked of Carpophorus, "How do we know that you will keep your word and spare the children?"

"You don't, said Carpophorus frankly. "But what have you got to lose? The kids will be killed anyhow."

The rabbi said sadly, "It is true," and addressed the people. More cries and sobs went up while Carpophorus listened with increasing restlessness. Finally the rabbi said, "Select the children you will spare, if being sold into slavery is to spare them." He turned away, unwilling to watch the sight.

Carpophorus approached the crowd. The worried mothers pushed their children forward, anxiously smoothing their hair in place, wiping their noses, and trying to twitch their rags into some semblance of neatness. Carpophorus made his selections rapidly. The mothers clung to the children, rejected and selected alike, sobbing over them while the children stared at Carpophorus curiously and tried to finger his soft tunic and glittering belt buckle.

Carpophorus called the guard and told him to make sure that the two groups didn't mix. Then he went to find the Master of the Games.

The Master was supervising the rebuilding of the inner barrier. This time the barrier was constructed of plaster boulders to represent the Masada hills. A model of the principal city, originally built by Herod the Great about 50 B.C., was cleverly incorporated among the artificial rocks. The scenery used in the shows was so elaborate that not even the vast storehouses under the Colosseum could hold it, and these props had been kept in rooms under the Temple of Venus nearby. The lions would enter the arena through openings among the rocks as though issuing from their lairs. The remnants of the Meridiani were still fighting in the arena to amuse the mob while the work was going on.

Carpophorus explained his deal with the Jewish prisoners and the Master nodded abstractedly while watching the work.

"That's all right. We'll still have plenty of prisoners to make a good show. The extra children can be killed by baboons later. Are many of them little girls?"

Carpophorus fidgeted uncomfortably. "I promised the old priest that I'd have them sold as slaves."

"You promised? Do you think a damn bestiarius is running this arena?"

"I swore to them by my gods."

"Well, unswear then. Do you think an oath to rebels counts with the gods?"

"Why not? I'm a Roman freeman. Before the gods, my oath is as good as the emperor's."

The Master looked at him curiously. "You're not getting soft in your old age, are you? All right, I'll see what I can do. But remember that I'm running an arena here, not a slave market. Start loading the lions into the barrier wall."

Carpophorus glanced up at the stands. The podium was filling up again as the patricians returned from their noonday meal. The Master shouted to the Meridiani: "Finish it up there, or I'll get some action out of you with the hot irons." Carpophorus went off to attend to the loading.

The lions were kept in far better quarters than the prisoners. The cells that contained them (still visible in the Colosseum) were inside the podium wall but below the level of the arena. Each cell was about eight feet deep and seven feet square. A water channel ran before the cells so the animals were sure of a constant supply of fresh water. The lead pipes and bronze turnkeys of these systems are still functional. Directly above the cells and on a level with the arena floor were a series of passageways so the slaves could race around on their various chores without disturbing the beasts. From these upper passageways down to the cells were narrow openings through which burning straw could be thrust into the animals' cells to force the inmates out into the lower passageways. From hence they were driven up ramps, covered with herringbone paving to give the animals a better grip, to the arena.

Carpophorus went to the second level to check the cells. The door of each cell was an iron grill that could be swung back on a hinge against the wall of the lower passageway. The door was nearly as big as the whole side of the cell so that the animal, panic-stricken by the burning straw, would have no trouble finding the opening and be able to rush out into the passageway before he got badly burned or suffocated by the smoke. As soon as he was out of the cell, the iron grill door was slammed shut after him and the movable barrier was shoved along the passageway, forcing him up the ramp toward the arena. By this system, a whole line of cells could be opened almost simultaneously by slaves stationed by each door and then the animals rushed to the arena. How the slaves caught between the animals and the movable barrier got out of the way in time I haven't been able to figure out. Probably a lot of times they didn't. But slaves were cheap.

Carpophorus didn't want to keep the lions in the cramped spaces provided for them in the barrier cages any longer than was absolutely necessary. On the other hand, as soon as Domitian returned from lunch and settled himself in the royal box, he would give the signal for the afternoon games to begin and those lions had better start pouring out of the barrier wall when he waved his royal hand. As Carpophorus went along the passageways, he passed slaves standing by the massive bronze sockets (still there) which held the windlasses to haul cages up the ramps and work the elevators. After making sure that the slaves were ready with the straw in the upper passageway and that there was a man by each grill in the lower section, Carpophorus returned to the arena level. The patricians were back in the podium, including the foreign nobility who had obviously taken advantage of the break to get well liquored up. The young editor was also in his box. Carpophorus reflected that the young patrician looked in worse shape than did the Jews who'd spent a week in the underground cells.

A frantic slave rushed to him. "Where in Venus' name have you been? The Master of the Games is furious. The emperor is coming through the passage that leads to the Baths of Titus and the lions aren't in place. The Master says that if you don't . . ."

Carpophorus didn't wait to hear the rest. The emperors had had three underground passageways built for their convenience, connecting the Colosseum with the palace, the baths, and the Lateran hill. You never knew which one they'd use. As Carpophorus raced down the passageways he shouted to the slaves in the lower level to open the cell doors. Immediately came the clang of the iron gratings being flung back and the slaves in the upper passageway fired their straw and thrust it down the holes.

From below came roars, snarls and strangled gasps as the burning straw fell into the cells, then the crash of the grills being slammed shut followed by the creak of the barrier being pushed forward and fresh snarls from the desperate animals. The lions were being herded onto movable platforms like freight elevators that would take them up inside the inner barrier in the arena. As the lions from each line of cells were pushed onto the platforms by the movable barrier behind them, the slave gang boss gave the signal, the slaves started turning the windlasses, and the animals were hoisted up inside the line of artificial rocks above them.

A slave watching from an opening in the podium wall gave Carpophorus a running commentary on what was going on above. "The emperor's coming into his box. He's stopped to speak to the Lady Livia. Now he's waving to the crowd. Now he's talking to that pinheaded kid he takes around with him. Now he's getting ready to sit down."

Carpophorus ran out through the Door of Death and dived into an opening in the plaster boulders. The lions were in the cages prepared for them, the movable platforms composing the cage floors. Now the lions had to be sprung out of these cages into the arena when the signal came.

Meanwhile, the Jewish prisoners had been introduced by another elevator into the model of the city which they had once called home. When Domitian gave the signal for the afternoon games to begin, the Jews opened doors in the sides of the model and stepped out into the glare of the arena. As Carpophorus had directed, they had been covered with animal skins. The captives were greeted by boos, insulting shouts, and cries. "Circumcised dogs! Traitors! Now see if your God can save you. Let out the lions!"

The backs of the cages in the artificial hill were movable and could be pushed forward to force the lions out into the arena. Doors were opened among the rocks and as the cage backs were shoved in, the lions began to pour onto the sand. Carpophorus watched anxiously through a peephole.

The lions slunk rather than walked into the area or ran with great leaps along the sides of the inner barrier, looking for some way to escape. Several of them sprang up, hung to the plaster rocks for a few seconds with their claws, and then fell back. Occasionally a lion running around the circle would suddenly turn and bump into the lion following. There would be angry snarls, lightning-like blows with the great paws and then the contestants would back away from each other to resume their anxious pacing. A few of them approached the crowd of people standing in the middle of the arena, studied them for a moment, and then turned away.

The children still with the group had begun to cry and several of the women had fainted. Some of the men were trying to sing a hymn but their voices faltered at the sight of the terrible beasts around them and the sound died away. A lioness circled the group nervously, unsure what to do. Carpophorus saw the old rabbi step forward and move his hands slightly as he had been instructed to do. The lioness only backed away. A young male with an orange mane had been scratching in the sand, either trying to find water or because he scented blood under the clean sand which had been spread over the arena after the last of the

Meridiani had been dragged out. He looked up and snarled at the rabbi. The rabbi took a few steps forward. After all, Carpophorus reflected, there was no reason why he shouldn't want to get the business over. What the people were suffering now was far worse than death.

The lion crouched down. Carpophorus watched the animal's tail. The man swayed slightly from side to side. Suddenly the tip of the lion's tail began to twitch. It's coming, it's coming, thought Carpophorus. Another step forward will do it. Why don't you take another step, you fool? He was tempted to shout to the man but restrained himself. His voice might frighten the lion.

Then he saw the lion gather himself together for the charge, digging in with his claws to get better purchase. The rabbi swayed again. So sudden was the lion's attack that he was on the man before Carpophorus saw him leave the ground. The rabbi fell and a scream went up from the crowd. The lion grabbed the man by the waist and ran with him as easily as a cat carrying a mouse, trying to find some secluded spot where he could eat in peace. A young black-maned lion from Nubia rushed forward and seized the man by the head. The women screamed again.

At the scent of blood, the other lions became restless. A lioness charged the closely packed group, bounded into the air and came down in the middle of them, striking blindly left and right. Two half-grown males, possibly her cubs, followed her. The crowd scattered like sheep when a collie rushes into their midst. The lions lashed out at them as they passed, more in fear than from hunger. A scream and a woman was down. Another scream and a child fell, his head smashed by one fearful blow. A full-grown male reared up and seized one of the men. The man's whole head vanished in the jaws. A woman was dragging herself across the arena with a half-grown cub clinging to her leg. The cub was shaking his head and growling, trying to pull the woman down.

Now Carpophorus could hear the insane, unnatural yelling of the crowd. As Petronius, the Arbiter of Elegance, remarked contemptuously, "These rag-pickers enjoy their carnival of blood." This yelling was not the usual cheering of an excited crowd during a chariot race, or the enthusiastic cries that greeted a skillful exhibition of swordplay. The pitch of the crowd's voices changed as does the cry of a pack of hounds when they see their quarry in front of them. Carpophorus knew that when the mob was in this mood, men and women had been known to hurl themselves into the arena in a frenzy of excitement and drink from the pools of blood on the sand. He knew that women in the stands were tearing long gashes in their cheeks with their fingernails and men were beating on the marble seats with their clenched fists until their hands were raw. The dull, pointless existence of the Roman mob would be unbearable unless their emotions were given some vent. For this purpose, the games existed. Death, torture, blood were the only spectacles that could really gratify the people's basic longing. They became drunk on suffering. Death and sex were the only emotions that they could still really grasp. The sight of a lion tearing a screaming woman apart gratified both instincts.

The Jews were dead. The lions had begun to devour the bodies. The corpses were jerked back and forth between the big cats and the sound of cracking bones was clearly audible. Carpophorus took his eye from the peephole. He knew what was coming next. These lions would not be saved as were the trained man-eaters and the arena must be cleared for the next act.

Ethiopian bowmen, magnificent in ostrich plume head-dresses, were forcing their way through the crowded aisles to balconies projecting over the edge of the podium. Even as Carpophorus turned away he heard the twang of the bowstrings and the roars of the stricken beasts. As he left the inner barrier, slaves were already rushing out with their hooks for dragging out the dead animals and humans, carrying baskets of fresh sand and jars of perfume to pour on the arena.

There was need for the perfume. On the podium, the patricians were holding sachets of scent to their noses and even the plebeians in the stands had covered their faces with handkerchiefs. In the, hot stadium, the blood and guts covering the arena sent up a fearful stench. Slaves were setting braziers full of burning incense in the stands, and the fountains were sending up sprays of saffron and verbena-scented water. Carpophorus noticed that the young editor of the games was standing up in his box, trying to crack jokes with the crowd to prove how democratic he was. The crowd good-naturedly kidded him back. So far, the games had been well up to standard and the mob felt friendly toward the young office seeker. But if the shows on the following days were not equally good, they would turn on him even though the youngster and his mother had bankrupted themselves trying to entertain the mob.

The inner barrier was hastily struck and the arena cleared for chariot races. These were to be novelty races, the real chariot races were held in the Circus Maximus which had been specially designed for them. To gratify the demand for racing. Domitian had increased the original four teams to six, adding Gold and Purple to the other colors. For the Saecular Games, he had staged one hundred races a day, cutting down the number of laps around the Spine from seven to five to speed things up. However, vast as the arena of the Colosseum was, it wasn't quite big enough for six four-horse teams to maneuver, so these races were more in the nature of a joke.

The first race was between chariots drawn by ostriches (called by the crowd "overseas sparrows"), the next by camels and the third by oryxes (African antelopes). As it was virtually impossible for the charioteers to control the animals, the results were an ungodly mess and meant to be. After the hysterical excitement of the massacre of the Jews, this interlude served as comic relief. Dwarfs in extravagant costumes ran alongside the chariots, deliberately frightening the animals, and pretending to get run over. One of the dwarfs got disemboweled by an ostrich kick—he forgot that an ostrich kicks forwards instead of backwards like a horse—and the crowd considered this accident the funniest of the whole show.

IX

By now, it was growing late and time for the main presentation of the day. As the sun dropped below the edge of the stadium, it became noticeably cooler and the sailors were sent aloft on the great masts to furl the awning. As it was pulled back, the overheated air rushed upwards, making the sailors' task more difficult as the vast expanse of cloth flapped wildly up and down but sucking in fresh air through the colonnade of arches surrounding the building; There were audible sighs of relief as the crowd relaxed, the slaves removed the braziers of incense which were unnecessary now that there was circulation of air, and the patricians put away their scented sachets. The podium was fuller than it had been at any other time during the day. Many patricians despised the usual run of the games, but now was the time for the gladiatorial contests, and even the most discriminating members of the nobility took an interest in them.

Led by a band, the gladiators marched into the arena, spreading out as soon as they reached the open sand so that they covered the entire arena. They saluted the royal box and the young editor who was betting desperately with everyone around him. The gladiators were the only part of the games which the sickly youth really enjoyed and, like all patricians, he considered himself an expert on manly arts. The crowd was wildly partisan, greeting the different units with shouts. "Hurrah for the Puteolaneans! Good luck to all Mucenans! The hook for Pompeians and Pithecusans!" Here and there fights started among members of different factions.

The gladiators made a stirring sight in their magnificent armor and accouterments. Trained to march in military formation, they swept across the arena keeping perfect step. Each group marched together with their special arms; the Hoplite in full armor, the Myrmillones with their curved scimitars, the Retiarii with their nets and tridents, the Paegniarii with their wooden shields and long bullwhips, the Essedarii coming last in their chariots with their lariat throwers beside them. There were many classes of gladiators and many types of arms, but the mob not only knew each class but also most of the individual men.

At this time, the gladiators were still a highly trained group of professional fighting men with tremendous pride in their calling. They had a great tradition to live up to. A hundred years before, Mark Antony's gladiators, whom he was training for a big battle in celebration of his expected victory over Augustus Caesar, had stayed by him after his troops had deserted. They had formed themselves into an army and tried to reach their master in Egypt, and when they could not find ships to transport them, had sent Antony a message urging him to return and let them defend him with their lives. Antony, however, had refused to leave Cleopatra. Other groups of gladiators had acted as bodyguards for emperors. An important gladiator was still the best known personality in the Empire. Horace wrote bitterly, "If Maicenas says it's cold today, it becomes the talk of Rome." Nero had asked to have his tomb decorated with carvings showing the victories of Petraites. Boys scribbled the names of famous gladiators on the walls of their rooms and innkeepers had signs up "Tetraites ate here" much as Sardi's has pictures of stage personalities on the walls.

But already the rot that was to overtake this bravest and most terrible of professions had appeared. It first manifested itself when gladiators were set to fighting wild beasts. Pompey had pitted gladiators against elephants. Claudius had cavalry fight leopards. Nero forced the Praetorian Guard to fight four hundred bears and three hundred lions. Neither the gladiators nor their lanistia managers knew when the men might be pitted against bears, lions or wild bulls at the whim of the crowd. As long as the bouts were man against man, there was a fifty per cent chance of survival—or say forty per cent allowing for men who died of their wounds afterwards. At that rate, it paid a lanistia to build up a great fighter like Flamma. But when men were sent out against wild beasts—unless they were trained bestiarii, who possibly ran little more risk than does a modern bullfighter— the casualties were ninety or a hundred per cent. Under those conditions, the enormous cost of creating an expert gladiator wasn't justified, any more than building up a boxer whom you know will be killed in his first or second fight.

As a result, anything was grist that came to the gladiatorial mills. Supposedly a man could be sentenced to the area only for robbery, murder, sacrilege or mutiny. But with the enor- mous turnover caused by the animal fights, the demand for gladiators far exceeded the supply. In the law courts, "sentenced to the arena" was the commonest of all verdicts. As the mob grew increasingly indifferent to good sword play, any criminal might have armor slapped on him and be thrust into the arena. Flamma would have been shocked at the exhibitions some of these men put on.

However, good fighting was still understood and appreci- ated by many of the mob. In the stands were old soldiers who knew how to handle a sword themselves, and the patricians in the podium had a traditional interest in fine fighters. Today, the young editor, or rather his stern old mother, was determined to put on a really good show, one that a descendant of Horatius might be proud to present. All the men in the arena were experts in their own line and there was to be no shamming. Nothing like that miserable exhibition that had taken place at the time of Caligula.

On this unfortunate occasion, five Retiarii had been matched against five Secutores. At that time, it was fairly common practice for gladiators to take a dive and the emperor would then give the thumbs-up signal. This trick preserved well-trained gladiators, and cut down the cost of the games. On this occasion, the Secutores defeated the Retiarii as had been previously arranged, for the whole match was as phony as a modern wrestling bout. The mob became so furious that Caligula decided to give the thumbs-down signal. At this double-cross, one of the Retiarii jumped up, grabbed his trident and killed all five of the Secutores who had their backs to him bowing to the crowd. The whole affair had been a public scandal, and the mob was still highly suspicious of any gladiator who dropped without obvious wounds.

After the parade, all the gladiators left the arena except the Retiarii and the Secutores. In the old days only one such fight was held at a time, but now fifty pairs were to fight together. The mob had come to regard gladiatorial combats mainly as an excuse for betting, so the more the merrier. The crowd considered the gladiators much as race track fans regard the horses: animated roulette balls or dice designed only for gambling. As man after man fell on the bloody sand, a groan went up from the losers and a yell of delight from the winners. An unknown gladiator might be spared if he held up his hand after putting up a good fight. He was only a long shot and no one had expected him to win. But heaven help a favorite who went down before the sword or trident of a dark horse. People had often waged their life savings on him and he had let them down. Then the stands were full of furious faces thrusting out their clenched fists with the thumb turned downwards, or stabbing at the prostrate man with an outstretched thumb. In such case, the young editor always followed the verdict of the crowd. He was putting on this show to get votes, not to antagonize the mob.

Carpophorus, his work finished for the day, strolled back to the Gate of Death to watch the fights. Near him, Negrimus, a Retiarius, was fighting Priedens, a Secutor. Carpophorus remembered the tip he'd given the guards on Negrimus and watched the fight with interest.

Negrimus threw his net and caught the Secutor, but before he could jerk the heavily armed man off his feet, Priedens had rushed forward still enveloped in the net and plunged his sword into the Retiarius' thigh. Negrimus went down but recovered himself, backing away from the Secutor still hampered by the folds of the net. Again Priedens struck, slashing his adversary on the left arm that gripped the net while the Retiarius tried to hold off the Secutor with the trident in his right hand. That portion of the crowd watching this particular fight yelped with eagerness as the Retiarius received a deep gash on the leg that crippled him. As the Retiarius relied mainly on agility to avoid the armored Secutor, Carpophorus supposed that the guards had lost any money that they might have wagered on his tip, but Negrimus managed to run his trident between the Secutor's feet and bring him down. Instantly Negrimus pinned his opponent to the ground with the trident, and then leaning with both hands on the shaft, looked to the editor of the games while the helpless Priedens made the sign for mercy.

The crowd voted for death and the young editor turned thumbs down. As the trident was a poor weapon which to inflict a mortal wound, the Retiarius usually dispatched his fallen adversary with a dagger thrust through the visor, but Negrimus had either lost his dagger in the scuffle or preferred not to use it. Instead, he called over a Secutor named Hyppolitus who had won his bout to kill the prostrate man for him. Priedens managed to struggle to his knees when the trident was removed and as Hyppolitus ran his sword into the Secutor's throat, Negrimus pushed him from behind onto the blade. (We know this bout happened, even to the names of the men and where they were wounded, as it is told in a series of pictures scratched on a wall in Pompeii. However, it happened in the Pompeian amphitheater rather than in Rome.)

Carpophorus was mildly pleased with the result, and determined to look up the two guards afterwards and demand a percentage of their winnings. As the other fights did not interest him and he was feeling the effects of his wounds, he returned to the spoliarium to have a drink and lie down. After this first bout, there was a full-scale battle between the Essedarii in their chariots, with laqueurii (lariat throwers) riding with them, and Hoplite infantry in armor and carrying spears. The Hoplites were Greek mercenaries who fought for hire under their own officers, either against an enemy or in the circus. On entering the arena, the Hoplites formed a closed phalanx, the equivalent of the British hollow square that broke Napoleon's chasseurs eighteen hundred years later. The phalanx was six men deep, the men in the last rank having spears twenty-four feet long, if we can believe Livy. How they were able to manage such long weapons Livy does not say. The men in the next rank had somewhat shorter spears, and so on to the men in the front rank who had spears only six feet long. This meant that the chariots were faced by a solid wall of spears and the front rank men were protected by six spears each.

The Hoplite did not stand in close order as might have been expected but at intervals of three feet apart, to allow the spears in the back to come through and give the men more room to handle their weapons. The officers stood inside the phalanx with drawn swords shouting orders. "Polybius, your spearhead is a good two hand's breadth out of line. Philip, keep your dress to the right. Epaminondas, you're not braced; a fly could knock you over in that position."

The Essedarii were using light, two-horse chariots. They galloped around the immovable phalanx with wild cries, suddenly swinging their horses in as though to force them on the spears and then whirling away again at the last moment. They were hoping to induce some of the younger Greeks to follow their motions with the spears, then the following chariot could dart into the opening thus formed, but under the iron discipline of the Hoplite officers the line of spearheads never wavered.

After a few false rushes, the Essedarii changed their tactics. They could not afford to tire their horses. There were two men in each chariot, the charioteer and the lariat man. As they came in again, the lariat man in the leading chariot built himself a loop by the spin known today as the Butterfly—that is, he spun a small loop vertically in front and to the left of his body. Then he brought it abruptly to the right and tossed the open noose toward one of the second tank Hoplites. If the Essedarii had been trying to catch a running animal he would have swung the loop several times around his head before making the throw to give him more control over the loop, much as a baseball pitcher winds up before a throw, but the Greek would have seen the cast coming and ducked or turned the loop with his spear.

This quick, unexpected, underhand toss was by far the better technique.

Even so, the toss failed. The loop struck the horsehair crest in the helmet of a front-rank man and was deflected. Instantly the Essedarii jerked his rope clear for fear that a Hoplite might grab it and pull it from his grasp. As the chariot thundered past, another Essedarii tried the same throw. He also missed, but in a following chariot still another Essedarii dared the overhead throw, knowing that the Greeks were concentrating on the other ropes. The long lariat snaked out over the ranks and settled around the neck of a man in the last rank. With an exultant whoop the Essedarii took a turn of the rope around a horn projecting from the rim of the chariot while the driver swung his team away and gave them their heads. The half-strangled Hoplite was dragged through the ranks, losing his spear and breaking the formation. Instantly half a dozen chariots rushed for the gap, the drivers yelling to their horses and beating the reins on their backs.

"Close ranks!" shouted the Hoplite officers, and the chariots were again confronted by a line of unwavering spears. All but one driver was able to swing away in time. The foremost chariot plunged into the spears. The horses screamed like humans as the spearheads plunged into their chests and they came down on their knees. The lariat man jumped out and ran, but the charioteer could not escape in time. He died as his horses had, with a spear through his chest.

Other chariots darted in to take advantage of the gap, hoping to break the phalanx before the Hoplites could disengage their spears from the bodies of the thrashing horses. The horses had been impaled on spears held by men in the third and fourth ranks. The officer in charge of that section of the phalanx took in the situation at a glance.

"Third and fourth ranks, kneel!" he shouted with lungs of brass. "Fifth and sixth ranks, three paces forward."

As one man, the third and fourth ranks dropped to their knees, elevating their spears as they did so and bracing the butts against the ground. The last two ranks took three measured steps forward to preserve the spear level. The oncoming chariots veered away.

The spears were torn clear of the kicking horses and the beast dispatched by an officer's sword with two quick strokes at the base of the animals' skulls. From the rear came the shouted order: "Fifth and sixth ranks, three paces to the rear—march! Third and fourth ranks, rise!"

The phalanx was itself again, ready to meet the next charge of the Essedarii.

Two chariots were coming in abreast now. Surely they intended to hit the phalanx full on, sacrificing themselves so the following chariots could plow through the broken line. The Hoplites braced themselves for the shock. At the last instant the chariots split, turning to left and right. The lariat man in the lefthand chariot threw his noose with the quick, underhand toss, aiming for a man in the rear rank. An officer cut the rope through with a single slash while it still hung poised in mid-air. He had served in the Near East and his sword was of Damascus steel. The other lariat man took advantage of the distraction. He had been playing his rope, doing a spin now known as the Ocean Wave, in an attempt to hold the Hoplites' attention and distract them from his friend. When he saw that his comrade's throw had been foiled, he instantly flung his own rope, leaning far over the side of the chariot and putting the whole force of his body into the motion, using his arm mainly to guide the rope. He caught a man in the fifth rank, jerked him off his feet, and began towing him through the other lines.

Among the Hoplites, homosexuality was regarded not only as natural but as an idealized and noble relationship between an older and a younger man. In the phalanx, the young men in the front ranks each had a lover among the older men in the rear ranks. This situation was believed to increase the efficiency of the regiment for no man would run away and forsake his lover in a crisis. But the relationship also posed difficulties. As the Essedarius dragged his captive through the ranks, the man's boy-lover dropped his spear and threw himself on his friend's body to save him. The two men together cut a wide swathe through the ranks. An officer passed his sword through the boy's throat and the cry of "Dress ranks! Dress ranks!" went up from the officers and the non-coms alike. But the damage had been done. The phalanx was broken, and the yelling Essedarii were charging in from all directions.

The commanding officer saw that the solid phalanx could not be saved, but there was one desperate expedient left. He gave the order, "Squads right and left! Open lanes and hold!"

The phalanx was divided into squads and each man knew his position in the squad as well as in the phalanx. The men on the right of the squads took two steps to the right and those on the left, two steps to the left. Lanes appeared through the phalanx through which the chariots raced. Before the Essedarii could recover, the commanding officer had snapped another order and the phalanx had begun to close again.

The commander of the Essedarii was a tough old experienced Briton, his red hair twisted into pigtails and his face and arms blue with tattooing. He had fought the Romans under the great warrior queen Boadicea and knew something about charging disciplined troops with chariots. He realized that if the phalanx was once allowed to reform it might never be broken again. Shouting his war cry, he urged his shaggy little ponies into one of the lanes and then, springing from the chariot, started laying about him with his battleaxe. Other Essedarii followed his example and within seconds the phalanx was broken up into little groups of desperate men fighting back to back against the charging chariots.

"Reform! Reform!" shouted the officers, but the phalanx could not reform. The men flinched from the plunging horses and were forced back into each other so that there was no room to wield their spears. The long spears of what had been the rear rank men were now useless and only the short spears of the front rank men could be employed. Attacked on all sides, no man dared to look over his shoulder for fear of being brained from in front with an axe or of finding one of the fatal lassos settling around his neck, but from behind him came screams and groans as his companions were cut down and at any instant he might feel a stab in the back as the Essedarii pressed in on the remnants of the phalanx.

The Hoplite commanding officer stood within a circle of his men who had turned at bay before the wild rush. Around them the rest of the Greeks were being massacred by the blood-splashed Essedarii. The savages' yells, their crouching figures, the delight with which they dispatched the wounded men, made them seem like Furies released from the pit. The fight was over, and in the stands the members of the crowd who had bet on the Essedarii were already yelling for the bookies to pay off.

The Hoplite general raised his voice in a last order. "From the Leuctrain wedge and forward!" he shouted.

The disciplined group around him broke their ring and with the general taking his position at the point of the wedge, moved forward behind their spears. It was a formation much like the old "flying wedge" in football—a triangle of men moving forward with increasing speed. Their spears were shortened and held close to their sides in the same direction as the point of the triangle. The wedge plowed through the Essedarii, picking up more of the Hoplites as it progressed until it became a formidable body of men against which nothing, could stand. The Essedarii refused to face it and ran for their chariots but the horses had stampeded. Dismounted, the Essedarii were helpless before the steady advance of the spear-men. The wedge swept around the arena, crushing all resistance and hamstringing the horses still attached to the chariots. When the Hoplite general saw all real opposition was over, he gave another order.

"Break ranks. Deploy and kill at will!"

With the first shout that they had given throughout the battle, the Hoplites broke their rigid formation and scattered over the arena. They paid no attention to thumbs-up or thumbs-down decisions and, indeed, the crowd was too awestruck by what they had seen to make any motion. One after another, the Essedarii were hunted down and speared. Then the Hoplites re-formed and marched across the arena towards the gate, heads back, chests out, the non-coms calling the step. They would leave Rome the next day to fight in the arena at Pompeii and from thence proceed to Africa to take part in subduing a Nubian chief who had revolted against Rome.

The Hoplites' victory was not popular with the mob. They despised Greeks as effeminate, and no one likes to have his illusions shattered. Besides, the Essedarii had won the favor of the crowd because of their picturesqueness and their unusual skill with the lassos. The Hoplites with their rigid discipline and haughty airs antagonized the rabble. Taunting cries of "Dog's-head, Dog's-head!" were raised to remind the arrogant Hoplites of the great battle of Cynoscephalae (Greek for Dog's-head) in which the forces of Greece went down in defeat before the Roman legions. The Hoplites paid no attention to the jeers. Only once did a Hoplite deign to reply to the taunts. A half-drunken man shouted, "Why don't you relax, Greek? The war's over!"

A young Hoplite officer glanced up at him. "Which one?" he inquired contemptuously. Then the Hoplites marched out through the Gate of Death still holding their faultless formation.

As a climax, a fight was staged with war elephants supported by two companies of the heavily armed Samnites. Thirty elephants took part in the battle, fifteen on each side, all carrying castles on their backs full of armed men. One group was composed of Indian elephants and the other of African. To the patricians and generals in the podium, this battle was of particular interest because it would prove, once and for all, whether the Indian or African elephant was superior for warfare.

The elephants were all males and had tusks. The females were useless for warfare as they would instinctively run from a tusked bull. Curiously, the African elephants were generally smaller than their Indian cousins although a full-grown African elephant is much bigger than an Indian one. This discrepancy was because the Indian mahouts were much more skilled at capturing and keeping elephants than were the Numidian mahouts. The Numidian animals were young bulls and many of them in poor condition.

All the elephants were heavily padded for protection. Most of them came from the government herd in Laurentum near Rome. The Romans occasionally found them useful for warfare, especially against a savage foe who would panic at the sight of the great creatures. It was the policy to spare the elephants as much as possible, both for reasons of economy and because the crowd disliked seeing them killed. When Pompey first exhibited an elephant hunt in the Circus Maximus, a wounded elephant had raised his trunk toward the crowd in the same appealing gesture that a fallen gladiator used when asking for mercy. The sight was so pitiful that even the brutalized mob rioted and the hunt had to be called off. (This gesture is apparently instinctive with elephants. J. A. Hunter, the famous Kenya professional hunter, told me that he has seen mortally injured elephants make the same motion when he moved in to finish them off. His native trackers refused to allow him to shoot, saying, "The elephant is asking to be allowed to die in peace.")

However, although it was the men rather than the elephants who were to die in this engagement, the elephants like every other living thing that entered the arena had to take their chances. The crowd watched, tense with excitement, as the two groups approached each other, the elephants trumpeting as they saw what was ahead of them and curling up their delicate trunks to keep them out of harm's way.

The Indian mahouts sat astride their elephants' necks while the Numidians rode sidesaddle; that is, sat sideways on the necks. The Indians used an ankus to control their mounts, a goad with a curved end like a fishhook. The Numidians' goads were shaped like the letter L. We know these details from a study of the coins put out to commemorate the fights with pictures of the different types engraved on them.

There were three armed men in each howdah, or "castle" as the Romans called them, on the elephants' backs. As the two herds rushed together the elephants used their trunks to pull the opposing mahouts off their perches. If they succeeded, the battle was won, for an elephant without his mahout would not fight and simply turned tail. When this maneuver was not successful, the two elephants fought with their tusks, giving angry gurgling cries and each trying to plunge a tusk into his opponent's soft belly. Meanwhile, the men in the howdahs hurled javelins at each other or tried to pick off their opponents with arrows.

One of the young African elephants was the first to flee. Buffeted and gored unmercifully by his bigger, better trained Indian adversary, the young bull could take no more. He turned and ran, pursued by the victorious Indian bull. As he dashed around the arena in terror, the howdah came loose and the occupants were flung to the sand. Directed by his mahout, the Indian bull stopped the chase and turned on the men. Each war elephant had his own special technique for killing men and once he had killed a man, he would always afterwards use that same method no matter what the circumstances. This bull grabbed the men with his trunk and then impaled them on his right-hand tusk. Other victorious elephants were kneeling on their victims, trampling them, or picking them up with their trunks and then throwing them on the sand or against the podium wall.

Meanwhile, the two companies of Samnites had broken into small groups and were following the elephants, sheltering themselves behind the great beasts to avoid the hail of javelins and arrows as modern troops often go into battle under cover of a tank. Once the attack had joined, the Samnites went into action, trying to hamstring the opposing elephants with their swords or rush under the animals and plunge spears into their vitals. The men in the howdahs protected their mounts as best they could. Sometimes they were not successful. One elephant dropped stone dead, killed by a javelin-hit in the eye. Another bull, hamstrung by the Samnites, continued to fight on his knees, grabbing the shields of the Samnites who closed in for the kill and tossing them into the air until he was surrounded by a circle of shields. The applauding mob gave the thumbs-up signal that this heroic animal might be spared, but a crippled elephant was worthless and a well-thrown javelin finished him off.

In spite of the efforts of the Numidians, the African contingent was going down to defeat. The Indian mahouts had pulled several of their elephants out the fight, and the elephants were picking up thrown javelins from the sand with their trunks and handing them up to the men in the howdahs. The Indians re-formed and prepared to finish the battle. But here came an interruption, the first one of that long and bloody day. Domitian, after a hurried parley with the generals who shared the imperial box, instructed the young editor to stop the fight. There was no longer any question in the minds of the high brass watching the combat that the Indian elephants had proved their superiority, and there was no point in killing more of the valuable animals. The crowd, generally so bloodthirsty, applauded the decision. The Romans liked elephants. Later, Commodus would amuse himself by killing three elephants in the arena, probably by shooting them full of arrows from the safety of the royal box, but at the time of Domitian there was still some lingering feeling of sportsmanship, especially when it involved such a huge, noble animal.

The elephant fight concluded the first day's entertainment. It was growing dark and torches had been lighted in the wall brackets. The crowd trickled out of the vast stadium, tallying up losses or winnings, arguing over the events, making plans for the morrow, and quarreling as they tried to force their way through the packed entrances.

X

After checking to make sure that his beasts were cleaned, fed and watered, Carpophorus went to Chilo's tavern near the Via Appia to discuss the day's events and drink himself into a blind stupor before the trials of the next day.

Each of the different professions attached to the circus had a certain wine shop it frequented, and outsiders were not encouraged to intrude. Chilo's catered to the bestiarii. The shop was several paces from the main highway, up a dark alley and near the "Wolf Den," as the Romans called the red-light district. When Carpophorus entered, he saw to his surprise and disgust that there was a distinguished company; the Master of the Games was sitting at one table and there were also a number of wealthy patricians, each with a gladiator bodyguard. The patricians were wrapped in cloaks and were ostensibly incognito although, of course, everyone knew who they were. Many of the patricians were connoisseurs of the games and the present group specialized in bestiarii. Although these aristocrats could make or break him. Carpophorus only gave them a surly nod as he sat down.

The walls of the inn were decorated by crude paintings, one of which was a copy of the fresco on the monument at Minturae to the eleven gladiators who had killed (and were killed by) ten bears, while another was a portrait of the famous venator, Aulus, inscribed: "To my good friend Chilo in memory of many a pleasant evening, Aulus." The inscription, however, had not been written by Aulus himself as he was illiterate. Another painting showed two men being thrown out of the inn, with the caption: "Watch yourself or you'll get the same."

Carpophorus shouted for wine. Chilo, a plump Greek, answered the summons. Chilo had been, by turns, a bandit, a fence for stolen goods, a beggar, and a cageboy at the arena. In addition to his present profession as innkeeper, he also pimped for the bestiarii and robbed travelers after slipping them a Mickey Finn composed of belladonna and hemlock.

"That was a fine show you put on with that tiger," remarked the fat Greek sociably. "How about some good Rhodian wine to celebrate. Just got a shipment in from Greece."

"I wouldn't use your damned resined wine to clean out a cage," retorted the venator.

"What do you want, a hundred-year-old Falemian?" demanded the Greek, stung by this insult to his native wines.

The innkeeper was made bold by the presence of the patricians and their gladiators. Carpophorus raised his head and stared at the man.

"Give me wine," he said slowly and distinctly. Chilo opened his mouth to retort, thought better of it, and pulled one of the long wine jars out of a hole in the counter top. Holding it by the two handles, he rested it on the pouring block and filled an earthenware cup. Carpophorus drained it at a draught and the innkeeper filled it again.

One of the patricians spoke up. "My friend—er, the cobbler here," everyone smiled for the friend was a well-known senator, "and I were discussing which was the more dangerous antagonist—a lion or a tiger. What is your opinion?"

Carpophorus was about to tell the man to go jump in the Tiber but restrained himself and answered the question civilly. Several other patricians entered the argument, some of them asking not too unintelligent questions. Carpophorus, after they had stood him several drinks, began to feel more friendly.

The Master of the Games remarked quietly, "That was a brilliant job you did, getting those raw lions to kill the Jewish rebels."

"Aw, you just have to know your lions and your Jews," said Carpophorus, pleased with the praise.

"Still, it was a fine piece of work. We have fifty zealots who are to fight seventy bears day after tomorrow, the zealots using only their daggers. That should be a good show."

"Haven't you got any prisoners except Jews?" demanded Carpophorus irritably. For some reason the memory of the old rabbi moving out to bring on the lions' charge bothered him.

"Thank Hercules for them," said the Master sincerely. "They built the Flavian amphitheater, they were the first people to die there, and they're still our main source of supply with their constant revolts. These damn Nazarenes or Christians or what-ever they call themselves are no good—die like sheep without fighting. I refuse to use them, myself."

Everyone nodded agreement. The group would have been considerably surprised if they could have foreseen that the Colosseum would be preserved only because of the edict of Pope Benedict XIV who wished it to remain as a shrine to the Christian martyrs—although comparatively few Christians ever died there; the great Neroian persecutions were in the Circus Maximus.

One of the young patricians was a friend of Titus, the juvenile editor giving the games. This adolescent lordling had been drinking too much and now burst out in praise of his friend. (This speech, by the way, is taken from the "Satyricon" of Petronius.)

"The next three days ought to be really good—no cheap slave gladiators but nearly all the fighters freemen. Good old Titus has a heart of gold and a hot head—the boys will have to fight it out and no thumbs-up. Titus will see that they have sharp swords and no one backs out. The arena will look like a butcher's stall before the day's over. Titus is lousy rich. Suppose he does spend four hundred thousand sesterces a day on the games, his old man left him thirty million so why should he worry? These games will make his name live forever. He's got some fine chariot horses and a female charioteer and Glyco's boy friend who's going to be tossed by a wild bull. Glyco found the youngster knocking-up his mistress. It wasn't the kid's fault; he was only a slave and had to do what the woman wanted. She's the one who ought to go to the bull, but if you can't beat a donkey you have to beat his pack, I suppose. Anyhow, it'll be a good show. What did the other candidate for magistrate give us? A lousy show with stinking gladiators—if you farted you could knock half of them over. I've seen better bestiarii, too. The shows were staged at night by torchlight; what did he think he was giving us, a cockfight? The gladiators were either knock-kneed or bow-legged and the substitutes for the dead men ought to have been hamstrung before the fight started. The only one to show any guts was a Thracian and the slaves had to burn him with hot irons to get him going. The crowd was crying. 'Tie 'em up!' for they were all obviously escaped slaves. Afterwards, the louse said to me, 'Well, anyhow I gave you a show.' 'You did and I applauded,' I told him. 'The way I look at it, I gave you more than I got.'"

Carpophorus was drunk by now as were most of the men. He shouted for food and the innkeeper brought him a steak. "I've seen bullock's eyes that were bigger than this," snarled the venator, hurling the plate to the floor. He grabbed for his wine cup and managed to spill it over the table. "More wine!" roared the venator, pulling himself to his feet by holding on to the bar. "More wine for the greatest man in the empire! I'm greater than the emperor, you know why? That son of a diseased sow couldn't hold his throne a week if it wasn't for men like me. Who was it who broke the Lucius Antonius mutiny? Me! I arranged to have forty little blonde girls all under ten years old raped by a band of baboons. The soldiers stopped the mutiny to watch the show. And what about the time lightning struck the Capitoline Temple, a very bad omen? The mob rioted and would have wrecked the city if I hadn't staged that chariot race, using naked women instead of horses. What's that dog's-dung, Domitian, ever done? I'm running this empire and I can lick any man in the house!"

An old bestiarius sitting in a corner cackled obscenely. He looked like a mummy, hairless, and eyes so sunk into his head that only the sockets showed, his, skin taut against his bones.

"Ah, you bestiarii are nothing but geldings today," screeched the old man as he gummed his winecup. "In my day, we were men. I made the sand smoke under me, I can tell you. We fought aurochs with swords and . . ."

"Hold your noise, you old wreck," bellowed the venator. "I know you old-timers—a lion, to hear you talk; and a fox, to see you act. None of you were worth your own dirt. Look at you now!"

"Yes, look at me now!" screamed the old man. "Wait 'til you're too old for the arena and have eaten your clothes and can't even get employment as a cageboy. I've seen you in the arena. You run around like a mouse in a pot. In my day . . ."

He got no further. Carpophorus had rushed across the room and seized the old man by the head and throat. Instantly half a dozen men threw themselves on the rabid Venator while Chilo rushed up flourishing a heavy wooden stool. He brought it down with all his strength on Carpophorus' head, but before the venator was knocked out, he had twisted the old man's neck in the grip he had learned in the arena. There was a sharp crack as the aged bestiarius dropped lifeless to the floor.

"The Watch! The Watch!" shouted a dozen voices. Into the wine shop strode a young centurion in gleaming armor followed by a squad of soldiers with iron-tipped staves.

"What's going on here?" snapped the young man. "Chilo, you'll lose your license for this. Who's this man? By Mars, it's Carpophorus! Throw some water on him—I have fifty sesterces riding on the bastard for tomorrow's games."

"He killed a man!" shouted Chilo, dancing in agony.

"Who, this old sack of bones? Don't lie to me, Greek, the man died of a stroke. Here, Telegonius, drag the corpse out and have it thrown in the Tiber. Keep better order, Chilo, or you'll find yourself in the arena one of these days. See that Carpophorus is ready for the hunt tomorrow afternoon or it'll go hard with you."

Several bestiarii carried Carpophorus to the nearest baths where expert masseurs kneaded him back to life, a feather was thrust down his throat to make him vomit up the wine, and a doctor patched his head and resewed the tiger scratches which had begun to bleed again. By next morning, Carpophorus was back at the Colosseum, feeling as though his mouth was the Cloaca Maxima, but able to enter the arena.

XI

The arena had been flooded during the night with salt water carried from the port of Ostia. (And how the Romans even with their unlimited manpower and wealth were able to accomplish this miracle I can't imagine.) The arena had been transformed into an enormous aquarium full of "sea monsters"—I suppose sharks and giant rays. Sicilian sponge divers with knives between their teeth dove from the podium wall into the artificial lake and fought the monsters. Afterwards, there was a nautical engagement between two fleets of galleys, one fleet sailing in by way of the Gate of Life and the other through the Gate of Death. While the arena was being drained, a seal act was put on: the seals barking in response to their names and retrieving fish for their masters. Then a bullfight was staged on the soggy sand.

The bulls were aurochs, a species of wild cattle now extinct, musk ox and the European bison. The Romans perfectly understood the difference between these animals, having seen them many times in the arena, but as late as the eighteenth century naturalists were still confusing the different species. The aurochs somewhat resembled the longhorned cattle of the old West except that they were considerably heavier and had short beards. An old bull's horns might be over six feet long. The

European bison is much like his American cousin but rather smaller. The musk ox are the same. Bullfights were first introduced into the games by the Emperor Claudius because they were comparatively cheap. Probably even semi-wild animals could be driven to Rome by mounted men just as the wild longhorns were herded by cowboys or the modern Spanish fighting bulls can be herded by mounted men with wooden lances. As long as the animals remain in a herd, they are fairly docile. Only when a single animal is cut off from the group does he become savage.

When the wild cattle first entered the arena, they were thrown dummies to toss. This trick put them in the mood to handle humans. Then the bestiarii dodgers entered the arena. The inner barricade to keep the animals in the center of the arena had been erected and burladeros (the Romans called them cochleas) such as are used in a modern bullring had been put up at intervals. The dodgers darted out from behind the shelter of these burladeros and rushed across the arena, encouraging the bulls to pursue them. An experienced dodger could tell without looking back how far the bull was behind him. If he had a lead, he'd slow down to make it look good. When the bull began to catch up, he'd put on a sudden sprint to reach the burladeros. As the man slipped behind the burladeros, the pursuing bull would often hit the wood with his horn, sometimes knocking off a large splinter two or three feet in length. One such splinter shot into the stands and killed a spectator.

Often two dodgers would work together, "spinning" a bull by keeping one man at the head and the other at the tail while the animal whirled around trying to reach first one and then the other of his tormentors. This trick could only be played with an inexperienced animal. A bull who had been in the ring several times before knew the ropes and would concentrate on one man, but the dodgers could recognize such an animal almost immediately by the way he took up a stand and forced the men to come to him instead of charging about blindly.

After a few minutes of this work, the bulltumblers entered. They were both men and women, naked except for a loincloth. These performers were Cretans and were performing a traditional art which can still be seen in the frescos at Cnossus. I'll admit that most antiquarians doubt if Cretans ever performed in an arena but there are Roman murals, of men turning somersaults over a bull's back, and I don't think that there's any question that this was a fairly standard act. It's still occasionally done in modern rodeos. One man would distract the bull's attention while the other ran forward and grabbed the bull's horns, immediately springing up and putting his feet on the bull's forehead (aficionados will please remember that these were not Spanish fighting bulls but wild cattle). As the bull tossed his head, the tumbler would shoot into the air, turn a somersault, and land on the bull's back, instantly sliding off while his friends shouted and ran in front of the bull to keep him occupied. A variation of this stunt was to turn a back somersault and be caught by two waiting friends. A man with impetus of the bull's toss to help him could go nearly fifty feet. Usually the bull instead of pursuing the man would stop, shake his puzzled head as if to say, "Where did he go?" and charge another tumbler.

In all these stunts, the tumblers were more afraid of the bulls' hooves than their horns. If a man slipped he could often avoid the great horns but he could not keep the bull from trampling him. Then the animal's great weight crushed his lungs and ruptured his liver.

There were frequent fights between the animals. An aurochs bull approached one of the bison who was lying down. The aurochs snorted, pawed the sand, but would not attack. A dodger

---

ran between the two animals, inciting the aurochs to charge, but instead of the aurochs, the bison was enraged. He sprang to his feet and charged the man with a speed no aurochs could have equaled. The dodger ran for the burladero as he had never run before but the bison would have had him if the Aurochs had not attacked the bison. The bison whirled and tossed the aurochs, lifting him clean off the sand. When the aurochs landed, the bison gave him a quick, short thrust in the eye, breaking off part of the horn in the aurochs' skull. Then he spun away on his forelegs, not his rear, and trotted off leaving the mortally wounded aurochs dying on the sand. At this moment a wildly excited patrician lady tore off a valuable brooch and, for no reason except that she was mad with excitement, hurled it into the ring. Her escort, a young knight, sprang from the podium, ran to the inner barrier, vaulted it and retrieved the broach. But the bison saw him. The animal turned and charged, killing the man almost instantly.

The head dodger nodded toward the Master of the Games, who had been watching closely from the edge of the inner barrier. The animals were sufficiently excited now for the next step. Also, they were growing sullen. Except for the bison bull, none of them had succeeded in killing any of their tormentors and they were beginning to take up stands—called a querencia in modern bullfighting. Either the animals herded together or picked a section of the arena and stood there motionless. The dodgers and the tumblers could now do nothing with them until the animals had been given new confidence by a kill.

The condemned criminals who were to be killed by the animals to give them this confidence (in the bullring, horses are used for this purpose) were now driven into the arena. Among them was the pitiful young boy who had been Glyco's minion, or male mistress. The boy—he could not have been more than fifteen or sixteen—staggered out into the blinding light of the white sand, for the awning did not cover the central part of the arena and protected only the spectators. Glyco, sitting in the podium with his mistress, leaned over the marble balustrade and called to the boy. The youngster, hearing the familiar voice and hoping for a reprieve ran toward the sound. The motion attracted an aurochs which promptly charged. Just before he struck the boy, the lad was jerked into the air by an invisible wire that had been tied around him before he entered the arena and was operated by the sailors in the overhead scaffolding. The boy soared into the air with a scream, only to be dropped almost instantly in front of a bison. The bison also charged, the boy was again pulled upwards, and this farce continued while Glyco and his mistress roared with laughter and the crowd howled its mirth. Eventually, either by accident or design, the boy was impaled by a charging aurochs. The long horn went completely through him and the bull charged madly around the arena, the shrieking boy pinwheeling around the horn with every shake of the bull's head.

When the criminals were dead, the dodgers and tumblers rushed out again. This time they were followed by Thessalian horsemen who galloped alongside the bulls, grabbed them by the horns, and then flung them down—bulldogging as in modern rodeos. Pliny describes this trick. Mounted men with lances also engaged the bulls while the venatores on foot, armed with swords and capes, also entered the arena. Carpophorus was one of these last.

Some of the wild cattle had been in the arena many times before. A pole vaulter made the mistake of trying to show his skill with one of these experienced animals. He ran toward the bull and when the animal charged, tried to vault over his head. The old bull simply stood back and waited for the man to come down. The expression on the man's face as he clung to the top of his pole put the crowd into convulsions. Carpophorus was armed with a javelin and seeing the vaulter's plight, stepped forward and drove his weapon into the aurochs' side.

He had meant the bull to drop dead instantly but his stroke missed and the wounded animal rushed away, tearing the javelin from Carpophorus' hand (a Pompeian fresco shows this scene). The bull wheeled and came back. Carpophorus, a venator rather than a dodger, could not avoid the rush. He went down between the bull's spreading horns.

The horns saved him. He clung to them while the mortally wounded animal smashed him repeatedly against the sand. Other venatores had run to his assistance. One of them grabbed the bull's tail (also in the frescos), another threw his cape over the bull's head, another plunged his sword into the animal's side. Between them they managed to drag Carpophorus to one of the burladeros. Even while they were carrying the wounded venator around the outside of the inner barrier to the Gate of Death, the bull followed them on the inside, watching the men. When they finally disappeared, the bull returned to the battle so suddenly that he caught the venatores following him. He tossed one man fifteen feet in the air, bounded around like a spring lamb while the man was coming down, and then gored him again. The venatores finally managed to get the corpse away from him and over the inner barrier. Then they stood back to let the mortally wounded animal die.

When the bull was sure the dead man was gone, he walked slowly over and stood sniffing the bloody sand as though it were incense. Then he looked up at the howling mob with quiet satisfaction and stood there proudly until his legs buckled under him and he fell dead.

Carpophorus had two broken ribs and the arena doctor had

to strap him up before he could go out for the next event. If you think that I'm exaggerating the punishment a man can take and still keep going, I'd like to mention that Camecerito, the famous Mexican matador, was carried from the ring after a bad goring and put on the operating table. When Camecerito heard the crowd yelling for the next matador who'd been sent out to kill his bull, he jumped off the table, wrapped a towel around his belly to keep his guts from falling out, and ran back to the ring. He killed the bull and then fainted from loss of blood. Louis Procuna once drove eight hundred miles from Mexico City to Nuevo Laredo after a goring and when he arrived the floor of the car was literally awash with blood. He still fought. I don't know what wounds the Roman bestiarii were able to take but I do know that they fought in event after event and must have often received terrific injuries. They had to be tough to survive.

The next act had a popular tie-in. A few weeks before, a whale had been stranded at the port of Ostia and thousands of people had traveled down from Rome to see the monster. A mock-up of the whale was raised to the arena on one of the elevators and then a trap door opened in its side, allowing the escape of several dozen lions, bears, wild horses, wild boars, stags, antelope, ibex, ostriches and leopards. Meanwhile a number of seesaws had been placed in the arena, each with two condemned criminals in the seats. As the man on the bottom was sure to be eaten, the desperate efforts of the prisoners to out-seesaw each other provided great amusement for the crowd.

Then the bestiarii came out again. Some of them were swung back and forth in baskets. The baskets were hung by a pendulum arrangement and at the bottom of their swing were close enough to the arena so an animal could grab them. The bestiarii in the baskets could control the rhythm of the pendulum as a man on a swing can control his speed. The trick was to control your basket so when it reached the low point there wouldn't be an animal waiting for you. Venatores, entering the inner barrier by turnstiles or through swinging doors guarded by slaves who quickly barred them if an animal tried to escape, decapitated the ostriches by shooting curved arrows at them. These arrows must have operated on the principle of a sharp-edge boomerang although how they could have been shot from a bow beats me.

Carpophorus came on with a pack of fighting dogs which he had trained himself. Some of these dogs could only have been Tibetan mastiffs from the description and as the Romans were getting elephants and tigers from India, there's no reason why they couldn't have got dogs too. He also had boar hounds, much like a harlequin Great Dane except they had slender muzzles. He had some of the enormous Molossian hounds from Epirus and the Hyrcanians which were so savage that the Romans thought they must be part tiger.

Carpophorus' best dogs were British, the British dogs being universally admitted the best of all breeds for fighting. The British used them in warfare and the Roman legionnaires were terrified of the brutes. It is said that one of them could break a bull's neck. Unfortunately, we don't know what they looked like. They are described both as "enormous" and "not very big." Possibly they were like a Norwegian elkhound. Personally, I think that they were probably not bred basically for type but for courage as with the bull terriers used in pit fighting which may be almost any color and weigh fifteen pounds or forty-five pounds.

Carpophorus loosed these dogs and then went in with his spear. The dogs attacked any animal that their master indicated. The stags and antelope they killed by themselves, chasing the animal around the arena until it turned at bay, and then pulling it down. One deer fell on its knees before the royal dais as though imploring mercy. In response to the shouts of the crowd, Domitian spared the animal. The dogs surrounded the more dangerous animals, rushing in and snapping to keep their quarry turning so he could not attack any individual member of the pack. Only when Carpophorus moved in for the kill would the dogs take hold, grabbing the animal by the paws, muzzle or testicles to hold him long enough for the spear to go home. They were also employed to dispatch the last of the wild cattle. Certain of the dogs were trained to grab a bull by the nose and hold his head down for the fatal stroke. These dogs had under-shot jaws, elevated nostrils so they could continue to breathe without loosening their grip, and bowlegs; the ancestors of the modern English bulldog. Sometimes a bull would toss a dog. When this happened, handlers were ready with long poles to guide the dog into the arms of another handler who broke the dog's fall. One bull, left for dead, suddenly sprang up and killed a venator.

After this attraction, a number of fast-moving novelty acts were introduced. Women were dragged behind chariots and the hounds set on them. "Legendary pageants" were staged showing the castration of Alys. Hercules being burned alive on a pyre, and Mucius Scaevola having his hand burned off. A prostitute and her pimp gave an exhibition of the various positions of sexual intercourse but in the middle of an embrace, Carpophorus set the Molossian hounds on the couple and they were quickly torn to pieces. A robber was crucified and bears encouraged to jump up and tear the dying man from the cross. A man representing Prometheus was chained to a rock and a trained eagle turned loose to pull out his liver. By the time the eagle was done with him, Martial tells us, "his mangled limbs still lived although all the parts dripped blood and in all his body was nowhere a body's shape." A man dressed as Daedalus with wings tied to his shoulders was thrown from the top scaffolding. When he crashed on the sand, a wild boar was released to gore the corpse. A lion, who had turned on his trainer when beaten, was killed by a venator using a sword and cloak. "Although the beast won't take the whip, he learned to take the steel." A bear, trapped in the mountains with birdlime, was surrounded by a ring of bestiarii and whirled around on the bloody sand with lowered head until a javelin dispatched him. A pregnant sow was cut open by a venator's spear and the litter of piglets spilled out of her side onto the sand. One piglet even lived.

Under the direction of the bestiarii, animal fights of all kinds were staged: lion versus tiger, a buffalo versus an elephant. A rhino tossed a bull as though it were one of the straw dummies. Then he killed a bear, a bison and two aurochs in quick succession. Finally an elephant was sent against him. According to the story, the elephant picked up a sweeper's broom and blinded the rhino with the coarse bristles. The blinded rhino charged straight through the inner barrier and crashed into the podium wall. The elephant finished the stunned animal by trampling him, and was then given candy, by his proud mahout. At last, the legionnaire were sent to clear the arena with their shield wall and line of spears.

Now came a delightful novelty. Instead of having the crowd find their own lunch, by order of the editor catapults flung roast partridges and pheasants among the stands. Slaves dragged basketfuls of other fancy foods up and down the aisles, Then the catapults showered the crowd with lottery tickets. The holder of a lucky ticket might win a set of furniture, a suit of clothes, a sack of gold coins or a valuable jewel. To get in on the act, Domitian ordered that government lottery tickets also be distributed. A winner might get a merchant ship, a house, or even a large estate.

Some of the tickets were fakes. A man might get a ticket giving him a beautifully carved box. When he opened it, a hive of bees would pour out. Other people would find that they'd won ten man-eating bears, ten dormice, or ten heads of lettuce. As a joke, Elagabalus even had the catapults throw poisonous adders in the stands.

When distribution of the lottery tickets began, many people left the stands. The distribution was always the signal for a free-for-all fight, only slightly less bloody than the battles in the arena. Only the lowest members of the crowd cared to expose themselves to the riot. After the distribution was over, speculators flooded into the stands offering to buy sight unseen any of the tickets. Not knowing what they might get, many of the crowd sold their tickets without bothering to cash them in.

During lunch, there were a number of novelty acts. There was a dog race with monkeys as jockeys. There was a fight between big cranes and African pygmies, the pygmies armed only with sharpened reeds. Men fought huge pythons with their bare hands and snake charmers from the Marsi Snake Training School in Greece handled cobras. At the end, there was a fight between women and dwarfs. As Statius wrote, "It was enough to make Mars and the Goddess of Bravery split their sides laughing to see them hacking each other."

In the late afternoon, the gladiators came on again. Domitian had given permission for the court gladiators to take part in the games. These men were all freemen, fighting for hire, and made a magnificent show in their golden armor and waving peacock plumes as they entered the arena. Their armor was solid gold, embossed with scenes of gladiatorial combats done by the leading artists in Rome. Julius Caesar provided solid silver armor for his gladiators; Nero topped him by giving his gladiators armor made of carved amber. Now Domitian had tried to surpass both men by arming his gladiators in gold. I don't know how many of these gladiators there were, but Trajan had five thousand pairs of gladiators fight to the death to celebrate his victory over Decebalius in 106 A.D.

These men were too important to use up in a general melee. Individual combats had been arranged. The crowd knew virtually every man in the outfit and cries went up of "Tetraites! Primus! Pamphilus!" We know these men's names for their tombs still remain with a carving of the gladiator, usually holding a palm in one hand as symbol of victory and his sword or trident in the other.

For these individual fights, unless they were between a Retiarius and a Secutor, a referee drew a line in the sand with his staff to mark the point where the two warriors were to meet. The two gladiators stood on either side of the mark while the referee gave the men their final instructions and slaves held their helmets and shields. The gladiators not fighting lounged under the statues of Victory which lined the podium walls.

The signal for the fight was given by a trumpeter, using a curved instrument like a French horn. The two men came together slowly, their faces obscured by their visored helmets, almost completely covered by their huge curved shields. Hucksters selling souvenir glasses and small trays with the pictures of the gladiators painted on them moved through the stands. The crowd stopped breathing as the arena was filled with the clash of steel for many of the spectators had wagered all they owned and possibly, their liberty on the outcome of the fight.

One man staggered. He recovered himself but blood was staining the golden armor. From fifty thousand throats came the shout "Habet!" (He's wounded!) Some shouted the word gleefully, some in despair, depending on how they had placed their bets.

The wounded man fell to his knees. His opponent pressed in on him, using his shield and the full weight of his body to force the injured man down. The gladiator fell and made the sign for mercy as a great shout went up from the stands. Few people bothered to give either a thumbs-up or thumbs-down decision; they were too busy either paying off or collecting their bets.

Another pair entered the arena and still another. As the fights went on the crowd stamped with enthusiasm, howled with rage, clapped with delight or flung miracles of insults at the fighters. There were constant cries of "Good! Aim for breast! What's the matter with you, you filth-gorged privy maggot! Let him have it! Give it to him!" When one man went down and the victor turned to face the stands, the crowd went into a frenzy of delight, especially if they had been betting on him. Women especially broke into hysterical spasms, and not only the common women in the upper tiers. The noble ladies on the podium often lost their heads. When one handsome young Myrmillo, only a few weeks before a simple farmboy living on the slopes of Apennine, paraded before the podium with his bloody sword upraised a great lady screamed uncontrollably and flung her brooch and necklace into the arena. Then she stripped off her rings, tossed them onto the sand, and finally ripped off her undergarments and threw them also. When the young Myrmillo came on the crumpled garments, he thought that the lady had simply thrown him her scarf or cloak. As he picked up the clothing to toss it back, the underwear unfolded. The simple boy stood gazing horrified at what he was holding. Then he dropped the garments and fled from the arena "more terrified of a woman's underwear than he had been of his enemy's sword." The crowd thought this was killingly funny and nearly died laughing. The patrician lady's husband was not so amused.

At that, he was more fortunate than the husband of Hippia, a noble lady who left her husband and children and fled to Egypt with a gladiator named Sergius. Juvenal says bitterly, "Sergius was maimed, getting old, had a battered face, his forehead was covered with welts from his helmet, his nose was broken and his eyes were bloodshot. But he was a swordsman!" Whether Juvenal intended any pun, I don't know. Many great ladies enjoyed the company of famous gladiators in their private apartments, but few ever ran off with their lovers.

Retiarii and Secutores were fighting now. One of the Retiarii was wearing a visored helmet which concealed his face; a very unusual uniform for a net-man. The Secutor was a steady old fighter while the helmeted Retiarius was a clumsy, nervous young man obviously unsure of himself. Suddenly the Secutor took a quick step under the circling net, knocked the trident out of his opponent's hand, and threw him down. The angry crowd contemptuously gave the death signal, which the editor instantly duplicated. The despairing Retiarius tore off his helmet and stretched out both hands in supplication to the crowd. A horrified gasp went up. Everyone recognized the young man as Gracchus, a descendant of one of the noblest of the great patrician families. A drunkard and spendthrift, the young patrician had been abandoned by his family, and sinking lower and lower had finally ended in the arena as a professional gladiator.

Unflinchingly, the Emperor gave the death sign, but the Secutor shrank from killing one "so noble and so vile." Amid a dead silence, the young man slunk from the arena.

The fights continued to rage. Slaves pushing two-wheeled carts collected the wounded, for these men were too valuable to be burned by hot irons or knocked on the head by a hammer. The referees had trouble saving the wounded even when the verdict of the crowd was for them, for the victorious gladiator, mad with the excitement of battle, would often dispatch his defeated adversary on the spot. A mural in Herculaneum shows a referee trying to stop a Myrmillo from killing his help-less Samnite opponent.

When the crowd tired of the individual combats, companies of gladiators engaged. A platoon of Gauls fought a platoon of Thracians. Domitian was always a strong supporter of the Thracian gladiators; people became fanatical fans of certain types of gladiators just as they backed the Reds or the Blues in the chariot races. One excited man in the stands leaped up during the fight to shout, "Smear 'em, Gauls! Those Thracians may be the Emperor's pet but they can't stand up against you boys!" The furious Domitian had the offender dragged from his seat and thrown in the arena. Then he ordered Carpophorus to turn his Hyrcanian hounds loose on him.

After the gladiators had finished there were jousts between Equestres-mounted men on horseback in full armor with lances. The armor these men wore was not plate armor like the Medieval knight's but breastplates, visored helmets, and greaves on their legs. However, the Romans did know how to make jointed armor, that is, armor that can slide in and out like an armadillo's plates as a man moves. The Secutores wore such armor on their right arms. Possibly the Equestres were similarly equipped and may even have worn chainmail. Their lances were probably light like the lances used by the Light Brigade at Balaclava. I can't understand why the Romans didn't make more use of the Equestres in warfare. An armored man on horseback can handle almost any number of footmen as the Medieval knights demonstrated. After all, King Arthur lived only a couple of hundred years after the time of Domitian and may even have been a British governor trained by the Romans. He certainly used knights to good effect. But apparently the Romans always put their faith in the legions maneuvering on foot. It was a great mistake.

By the time the Equestres had finished their jousting, it was dark, but the games still continued. The catapults flung figs, dates, nuts, cakes and plums to the crowd. Free wine was distributed. Torches sprinkled with incense were lighted. The incense was of different kinds so the torches burned red, yellow, blue and green. Silver stars were hung from the awning. In the arena, cavalry fought against chariots and heavily armored Hoplomachi fought equally well-armed Provocatores, the vari-colored lights dancing on the sword blades and shields. At the end, the arena was flooded again for a fight between African natives in war canoes while barges full of beautiful nude girls floated around the podium wall, chanting songs and throwing favors into the stands.

XII

Marcus Aurelius, the great Roman emperor and philosopher, remarked: "I wouldn't mind the games being brutal and degrading if only they weren't so damned monotonous." Although the Romans devoted an enormous amount of ingenuity to ringing in variations, there is no doubt that Marcus was right. But the mob had developed a morbid taste for the spectacles which had to be gratified. Nietzsche believes that the great driving power which had made the Romans masters of the world had to be given a vent. With no worlds left to conquer, their force was dissipated in watching these holocausts.

So I'll only touch on some of the high points of the remaining four days of the games. A walled city was constructed overnight in the arena and besieged the next morning by legionnaires with battering rams, catapults and burning arrows. The city was defended by Persian troops. The Romans advanced under cover of their interlocked shields while the Persians threw down boulders, boiling oil and beams on the "testudo", or tortoise, as the formation was called. Under shelter of the testudo, other legionnaires rushed the wall with a battering ram, its head a carved ram's head made of bronze. Movable towers were brought up on rollers and drawbridges dropped from their tops over which the troops attacked. From other levels of the towers, catapults threw stones and clusters of javelins against the defenders. The legionnaires captured the city, but only after heavy losses.

Afterwards, there were fights with single-stick and quarterstaffs, the Paegniarii fought with their bullwhips, protecting themselves with their wooden shields, and the Postulati fought with, darts. To keep the crowd amused during the noon hour, women were tied to bulls and dragged to death and little boys assaulted by men dressed as satyrs. A confessed Christian named Antipas was put in a bronze figure of a bull and a fire lighted under the image. The man's screams came out of the bull's open mouth as though the animal were bellowing. Chimpanzees were made drunk on wine and then encouraged to rape girls tied to stakes. When these man-sized apes were first discovered in Africa, the Romans believed that they were genuine satyrs, the mythological beings who were half man and half goat. There were also man-size apes called tityrus with round faces, reddish color and whiskers. Pictures of them appear on vases and they were apparently orangutans, imported from Indonesia. As far as I know, the Romans never exhibited gorillas although these biggest of all apes were known to the Phoenicians, who gave them their present name which means "hairy savage."

There were also amusing touches, or what the Romans considered amusing. A jeweler who had sold some fake stones was sentenced to the arena. The wretched man was driven into the arena and a lion's cage rolled out before him. While the jeweler fell on his knees and prayed for mercy, the door of the cage was pulled back—and out walked a chicken. The jeweler fainted from shock while the emperor had the heralds announce: "As the man practiced deceit, he has now had it practiced on him." The jeweler was allowed to leave the arena alive. (This actually happened during the reign of the Emperor Gallienus in 250 A.D.)

The Romans had a robust sense of humor. At the time of Caligula, a gladiator had his right arm cut off so he was helpless. The crowd considered this uproariously funny. Another gladiator, named Bassus, strolled around the arena defending himself with a golden chamber pot. But at least one trick played by Caligula would seem to us today, if not funny, at least a grim form of poetic justice.

There was a group of people who used to wait under the stands by the passageway along which condemned prisoners were let to the arena. These people were degenerates of the most revolting type. They would follow the prisoners, pawing, spitting and mauling them while recounting the tortures they would soon face. The sight of the cringing wretches acted as a sexual stimulus to them. (Ilsa Koch, the wife of the German supervisor at Buchenwald, was a pervert of this same sort. She used to fondle the condemned prisoners being taken to the gas chamber as they were led past her.)

These perverts were a great nuisance to the guards in charge of the prisoners and strict orders were given to keep them away from under the stands, but somehow they always managed to bribe or force their way in. In their efforts to enjoy the suffering of the prisoners to the last moment, they crowded into the passageways that led to the podium and sometimes even onto the podium itself. On one occasion, Caligula gave orders for the guards not to drive them away. Delighted, the sadists flung themselves on a batch of prisoners headed to the arena, kicking and pinching them as the captives struggled along. These degenerates became so absorbed in their sport that they didn't notice where they were going. Suddenly they heard a gate slammed behind them and found themselves in the arena with the condemned prisoners! The perverts ran wildly up and down before the podium wall, screaming that they were

Roman citizens and that a terrible mistake had been made. After enjoying their antics for a while, Caligula ordered the wild beasts to be loosed and the perverts died with the others.

Not all the acts put on dealt with blood and sex, although unquestionably these became the main attractions. The Roman shows went through somewhat the same evolution as did burlesque in America. Originally, burlesque shows were a rough-and-ready sort of vaudeville featuring dancers, novelty routines, comedians and, of course, plenty of pretty girls although the girls were only a background to the feature acts. As the tastes of the audiences grew more crude, the girls became strippers and the whole show revolved around them. Burlesque, which had produced such great comedians as W. C. Fields, Fanny Brice, and Bert Lahr, finally featured comedians who did nothing but tell dirty jokes and only came on to give the girls a chance to change their G-strings. However, to break up the steady series of strip routines, there always had to be an occasional singer, an occasional vaudeville turn, a few dance teams, and so on.

In much the same way, the Roman mob had to be given some kind of break between the gladiatorial combats and the whole-sale slaughter of animals by the venatores. These "fill-ins" might be ballet dancing, little skits like our "blackouts," or exhibitions of trained animals. Apuleius describes one of the dances:

"A number of beautiful girls and boys in costume gave a Greek Pyrrhic dance. Lines of dancers wove in and out of circles, sometimes all joining hands and dancing sideways and then separating into four wedge-shaped groups with the base of the triangles making a hollow square. Then the boys and girls would suddenly separate and dance opposite each other."

The skits given in the arena were typical bedroom farces which have remained unchanged for two thousand years. A man and woman would be in bed. There's a loud knocking. "By gracious Vesta, it's my husband!" the woman screams. The man dives under the bed but the new arrival is only another of the woman's lovers. They get in bed and there's another knock. That man also dives under the bed and so on until the husband really does arrive. Then after some byplay, one of the lovers crowns him with a chamber pot and everyone runs out of the arena.

The trained animal acts must have been very remarkable. The Romans had an unlimited number of animals available for the games, and the bestiarii could select only those individual animals which showed promise—a long cry from today when a lion tamer, for example, has to take virtually any animal he can buy, borrow or beg. Also, the Romans had unlimited time and plenty of cheap labor for cageboys, trainer's helpers, and so on. They taught elephants to walk a tightrope, horses to dance on their hind legs and bears to pull chariots while another bear acted as driver. They also had trained ducks and geese as well as performing monkeys. The Thessalians had "bulls as well-trained as chariot horses" which would lie down, ride in chariots or fight each other on command. All these feats modern trainers can duplicate, but the Romans also taught lions to retrieve hares and bring them to their master's feet uninjured, after first having them kill bulls to prove their ferocity. They also staged special hunts: trained cheetahs (the African hunting leopard) coursing antelope, and caracals (African lynx) catching rabbits and partridges.

The Romans also exhibited unicorns. These animals were really oryx antelopes from Africa but the bestiarii would take a young oryx and bind his horns together as though grafting twigs. The soft young horns would grow together, producing one straight horn which was a far better weapon against other animals in the arena. The legend of the unicorn probably originated from this custom although some students believe that the original unicorn was the one-horned rhinoceros of India.

Individual fights were often staged between animals, and some of these animals became as well-known as the famous gladiators. Statius wrote a beautiful ode to a lion who was killed by a younger opponent in the arena at the time of Domitian:

"Poor fellow, what good has it done you to learn to obey a master weaker than yourself, to learn to leave and re-enter your cage on command, to retrieve your quarry for him and even let him put his hand between your jaws? Once you were the terror of the arena and all the other lions shrank back when you marched past. You died fighting, as bravely as any soldier, and even when you knew that you'd received your death wound, you waited with open jaws for the enemy to finish you off.

"Yet know that the people and the senate mourn for you as though you were a famous gladiator and among thousands of other beasts gathered from Scythia to the banks of the Rhine, Caesar's face only fell when you died although it was nothing but another lion lost."

There are accounts of trained lions being used to pull chariots for the editor of the games and also several cases when the trained lions saved their bestiarii masters from wild animals. Then, of course, there's the famous story of Androcles and the lion. Androcles was a Greek slave who escaped from his master and while wandering around the desert, met a lion with a thorn in his foot. Androcles pulled out the thorn and the lion never forgot the kind deed. Later, the lion was captured and shipped to the arena and so was Androcles. The starved lion was turned loose in the arena to devour the escaped slave but the lion refused to harm the man who had befriended him. A leopard was turned loose to do the job and the lion killed the leopard to defend his pal. The crowd demanded that both Androcles and the lion be freed. Afterwards, Androcles made a living by exhibiting the lion in taverns. Gellius and Aelian both swear to the truth of this story (it happened during the reign of Claudius) so I'll believe it. Ordinarily, I'd have my doubts. Anyhow, it's one of the best authenticated legends in history.

What happened to Carpophorus? I don't know so I'll invent an ending suitable for this strange man.

A wealthy noblewoman asked Carpophorus to bring one of his trained jackasses to her room at night, promising him a fabulous sum of money. Carpophorus naturally complied. The lady had made elaborate preparations for the event: four eunuchs had placed a feather bed on the floor, covered with Tyrian purple cloth embroidered in gold, and had arranged soft pillows at one end. The lady instructed Carpophorus to lead the jackass to the bed, get him to lie down, and then with her own hands rubbed him with oil of balsam. When the preparations were complete. Carpophorus was ordered to leave the room and return the next morning. This performance is described in great detail by Apuleius in "The Golden Ass."

The lady demanded the jackass's services so often that Carpophorus was afraid that she might kill herself but after a few weeks his only concern was that she might totally exhaust the valuable animal. Still, he made such a fortune from the business that he was able to purchase a genuine unicorn's horn. Of course, Carpophorus knew all about the oryx-unicorns used in the arena, but this horn was different. It was pure ivory and over seven feet long. There were only a few of these horns in Rome and they were enormously valuable because if poisoned wine were served in a cup made of a unicorn's horn, the poison would bubble and betray its presence. Carpophorus suspected that these horns were faked in some way, but after carefully examining his purchase he became convinced that it was real ivory and did not come from any known animal. The bestiarius' ambition was to find a unicorn and exhibit it in the arena.

Unicorns were supposed to be tropical animals, but Carpophorus discovered that these horns were imported from the Baltic. This, he decided, explained why the Roman animal catchers in Asia and Africa had never gotten any unicorns. He managed to scrape up acquaintance with the crew of a Viking ship that had come to Ostia to trade and do a little piracy on the side during the voyage home. The Vikings had some broken pieces of unicorn horns with them and Carpophorus was able to get one member of the crew drunk at Chilo's tavern. The sailor told him that the horn came from a great fish which fisherman occasionally caught in their nets. The Vikings called it a narwhal. The fish might be called a sea-unicorn for it had one long horn growing from the tip of its nose.

Carpophorus didn't swallow this yarn. The horn was ivory and fish didn't grow ivory. Still, he thought that unicorns might sometimes swim rivers and be caught in nets so that was how the legend started. He traveled to the Baltic with a "negotiator ursorum," a bear-catcher, but was unable to get any unicorns. But he got something almost as valuable—three great white bears unlike any he had ever seen before. These bears came in on icebergs near Ultima Thule, the last outpost of land to the north. Today we call it Iceland.

Carpophorus had the crazy idea that these bears must come from some great land lying to the west, for surely they could not spend all their lives on the floating icebergs. On his way back with the bears, he advanced this theory to a young centurion who was in charge of one of the frontier forts in Scotland built to keep the Picts and Scots from raiding down into Roman Britain.

"There is no land to the west," the centurion told him confidently.

"How do you know?" the bestiarius demanded.

"Because if there were, this damn government would have us legionnaires over there policing the place," said the centurion downing a cup of strong wine.

The bears made a great hit in the arena. The Roman writer Calpurnius describes how the arena was flooded and the bears dove into the water and fought seals. (Polar bears were exhibited in the arena, but at what period is uncertain.) But when the time came for the next act, the bears couldn't be moved. They were still eating the seals, and polar bears are mean animals to handle at the best of times.

The emperor motioned to the archers to kill the beasts for the shows ran on a strict time schedule. Carpophorus refused to see his precious bears killed. He plunged into the knee-deep water and tried to drive out the bears with his flail. Hampered by the water, he could not avoid the animals' angry rushes. So he died, as did most of his profession, under the teeth and claws of his savage wards. The Romans never realized that they held in their hands the clue to the discovery of a great new world.

XIII

You may wonder where the Romans got all the animals they used in the games. You'll wonder more after reading a few statistics. Trajan gave one set of games that lasted 122 days during which eleven thousand people and ten thousand animals were killed. Titus had five thousand wild animals and four thousand domestic animals killed during the one hundred-day show to celebrate the opening of the Colosseum. In 249 A.D., Philip celebrated the one thousandth anniversary of the founding of Rome by giving games in which the following were killed: one thousand pairs of gladiators, thirty-two elephants, ten tigers, sixty lions, thirty leopards, ten hyenas, ten giraffes, twenty wild asses, forty wild horses, ten zebras, six hippos and one rhino (*Rome and the Romans,* by Showerman).

Statistics in themselves don't mean too much so let's take some specific examples. The Emperor Commodus killed five hippopotami himself one day in the arena, shooting arrows from the royal box. Hippos were fairly common in the arena as this and other accounts show. After the Roman Empire fell, the next hippo to reach Europe was in 1850. A whole army division had to be used to capture the animal. Getting the hippo from the White Nile to Cairo took five months. The hippo spent the winter in Cairo and then went on to England in a tank containing four hundred gallons of water to keep it cool. Yet the Romans imported hippos wholesale for their games; in fact they actually exterminated the hippos in the Egyptian Nile. The Romans imported both the African and the Indian rhinoceros, and even the most ignorant members of the crowd could distinguish between the two beasts readily. Mosaics showing the capture of an Indian rhino have recently been uncovered in Sicily. The next Indian rhino to reach Europe was in 1515. Today, there are only six of them in captivity.

Whole territories were denuded of wild animals to supply the arena. The early Christian fathers could only find one good thing to say about the bloody spectacles—the demand for animals cleared entire districts of dangerous predators and opened them to farming. Several species were either exterminated or so reduced in numbers that they later became extinct: the European lion, the aurochs, the Libyan elephant and possibly the African bear. There are no bears in Africa today and most scientists believe that there never were any, but the Romans did get a "bear" from East Africa and Nubia. What was it?

We don't know, but curiously in Kenya today there is a persistent legend of a "Nandi bear," supposedly a very large and ferocious bear which lives in the Aberdare Mountains. It occasionally attacks natives and has been seen by a few white people although no specimen has ever been brought in. Recently, the site of a Roman "trapping station" has been found in this locality. Perhaps the Romans' "African bear" still exists.

Collecting and shipping these thousands of animals was an enormous industry. Wild animals were the most valuable gift a barbarian monarch could make to his Roman overlords and even Roman governors had to collect animals. There is an interesting and amusing series of letters between Cicero, a newly appointed governor of a province in Asia Minor, and Caelius Rufus, who was running for the office of aedile in Rome. Rufus wanted leopards for the games he was giving. Cicero was busy trying to administer his province and wasn't interested in catching leopards. Even before poor Cicero got to his province, he got a letter from Rufus: "Dear Cicero: please try to get me some good leopards . . . ten will do for a start. Tell your natives to hurry." When no leopards arrived, Rufus wrote: "My dear friend Cicero: In nearly all my letters I've mentioned the subject of leopards to you. It would be a terrible disgrace if, after Patiscus [a local Roman businessman in the same area] has sent me ten, you can't send me many more. I have those ten and ten more from Africa. If I don't hear from you, I'll have to make arrangements elsewhere." Later: "If I hadn't got some African animals from Curio, I wouldn't be able to put on a show at all. If you don't send me some leopards, don't expect any patronage from me."

Cicero wrote to a friend: "Another letter from Rufus . . . all he talks about is leopards." Then Rufus gave his games and got elected to the aedileship. Right away Cicero wrote him: "Dear, dear Rufus: I can't tell you how sorry I am about the leopards. I've put all the professional hunters to work but there seems to be the most remarkable scarcity of wild beasts at this time of year. But don't worry, I have everyone working on it and anything we get will be for you and no one else."

Rufus had a right to be annoyed. Sulla, who became dictator, freely admitted that the people had originally voted him into office only because he had a tie-in with Bocchus, an African monarch, and could get plenty of animals for the games. In search of animals, the Roman trappers went to Norway, where they brought back moose and elk: to Burma, for rhino, cobra and elephants; and to Lake Victoria in the heart of Africa. As today, Africa was the great trapping ground for wild animals. The Romans even exhibited African porcupines in the arena; naked boys had to catch them with their bare hands. Plautus, a Roman humorist, wrote: "By the gods, next they'll be giving exhibitions of trained African mice."

From various sources, let's create the character Fulcinius, a professional animal trapper whose territory was Africa. We can suppose that Fulcinius was a half-caste, the son of a Roman legionnaire stationed in Algeria, by an African mother. As today, half-castes were not popular with either race, and Fulcinius grew up a lonely boy, considering himself superior to his mother's people but knowing that he would never be accepted by Romans. Roman writers describe such a man as a "savage among savages, a shy, sullen man who hated society and was only happy in the jungle."

From his mother's people, Fulcinius learned the tricks of animal catching, which have remained unchanged to the present day. He learned how to dig a pit, surround it with a high wooden fence, and tether a young calf in the pit. When a lion heard the kid bleating, he would jump over the fence, fall into the pit and be caught. He learned how to direct natives to drive herds of antelope into rivers where they could be lassoed by men in boats, or herded down ravines covered with slippery rawhides so the animals would lose their footing and could be hogtied by waiting men. He organized hundreds of beaters to move in from all sides through a stretch of jungle, driving the animals into a smaller and smaller space. At last, Numidian spearmen with their great oval shields formed a wall around the captives and held them long enough so men with lassos and nets could complete the capture. Apparently even lions were caught in this manner. There's a picture of it in the Roman villa at Bona, Algeria.

The recently uncovered villa near the village of Armerina, Sicily, contains frescos—some of them sixty-six yards long—showing in great detail how animals were captured and crated for shipment. The villa is thought to have been the summer home of the Emperor Marcus Aurelius Valerius Maximianus who ruled about 300 A.D. That the emperor should have devoted so much space to pictures of capturing animals shows how vital this profession was to the Romans.

In one mosaic, mounted men are shown driving stags into a circle of nets, one stag having already been caught by his antlers. Another shows men loading elephants onto a galley while others drag an unwilling rhino calf toward the gangplank as trained dogs snap at the animal from the rear. Still others show a Roman animal catcher with a huge shield pointing to a lion who is eating an oryx he has just killed. The animal catcher is directing his Moorish assistants how to surround and net the animal. One mosaic shows a cart pulled by oxen with native drivers and on the cart is a big wooden shipping crate containing a lion or a leopard. An animal catcher walks beside the crate, steadying it with his hand. On top of the crate is a funnel-like arrangement which is often shown in these pictures. Unless it was used for pouring water into the cage. I can't imagine its purpose. A mural shows men carrying cranes onto a ship and two men are wrestling a hartebeest onboard. Others are carrying up the gangplank wild boars wrapped in nets and suspended from poles.

Fulcinius must have done all these things and many more too. He must have caught elephants by driving them into box canyons and, as he probably didn't have enough trained elephants to take them out, starved them into submission by giving them only enough barley water to keep them alive. He also hired Numidians to crawl among a herd and hamstring the mothers with their spears so the young could be captured. He caught chimpanzees and baboons by putting out bowls of wine and then picking up the animals after they were drunk. To catch pythons, he prepared a long bag made of rushes which he put near the snake. The snake was then driven toward the bag and thinking it a hole, would crawl inside. Then the cords closing the mouth of the bag were closed. When a "bear" (whatever the African bear was) was found in its den, nets were hung on the outside and the bear driven out with trumpet peals and yells. Nooses were set in game trails and animals driven into them. Along the sides of the trails, colored streamers were hung from lines so that the animals, alarmed by the strange objects, would stay on the trails and not bolt off into the bush.

Organizing these hunts must have been a tremendous undertaking. The catchers could demand that legionnaires stationed in their area help with the drives and the commanders had to cooperate, for getting the animals was crucial to the politicians in Rome. The whole civilian population could be drafted for this work and, as some of Cicero's angry letters show, this often crippled the local economy for many of these drives lasted for weeks.

As with all animal collectors, Fulcinius' main trouble was not in getting the animals but in shipping them. The animals had to be taken by ox cart to the coast or floated down rivers on rafts. This journey could take months. Fulcinius established way stations along the route where the animals could be released in large enclosures for periods of rest and exercise. According to Roman law, the villagers were forced to provide food for the animals, but collecting the food often proved so difficult that Fulcinius had to appeal to the local Roman garrison for help. If there was no garrison, he used his native mercenary spearmen who traveled with the animal caravans. These men were merciless. On one occasion they dug up corpses in a local cemetery and fed them to the animals. Fulcinius got frequent complaints from Rome but probably his invariable answer was: "Do you want the animals or don't you?" However, the situation got so bad that an imperial order had to be passed prohibiting animals being kept more than a week in any one resting station.

Even after the animals had been loaded on ships, the voyage to Ostia, the port of Rome, was a long and dangerous affair. "The sailors were afraid of their own cargo," wrote Claudian. The trip up the Red Sea was particularly treacherous because of the reefs and shoals. To make matters worse, the voyage had to be made at night and the ships tied up during the day to spare the animals from the heat of the sun.

As far as Fulcinius was concerned, a human life meant nothing compared to the successful shipment of the animals. Once when he was unloading cages on the docks at Ostia, a famous sculptor named Pasiteles set up his table on the dock and began making models of the lions. Fulcinius told the man to get out but Pasiteles refused. A few minutes later, a cage containing a leopard was smashed during the unloading and the animal nearly killed the sculptor. Fulcinius' only reaction was a blind fury at the sculptor for getting in the way. (This incident did happen although I don't know the name of the animal collector.)

It's rather interesting that some two thousand years later another animal collector made a great reputation for himself by capturing and importing animals under much the same conditions as did Fulcinius, supposedly for zoos but actually so fights could be staged between the animals in corrals and pits for Hollywood motion picture cameras. The pictures of these fights were so popular that they are still appearing in re-run theaters and on TV. If you want to know what the Roman arena must have been like, tune in on one of these programs. I saw one showing a fight between an African lion and an Indian water buffalo supposedly taken "in the heart of the Dark Continent." Of course, nobody cares whether the pictures are faked or not. Like the Romans, all they want to see is the fight. I've also seen pictures of "native spearmen fighting man-eating lions" which were staged by order of a local governor in Africa as a tourist attraction. The lions arrived in crates and the natives got their spears and shields through a European supply house. I've heard that three men died as a result of the fight. A good, average, arena spectacle.

How did a man like Fulcinius die? Probably of black-water or malaria fever. Or perhaps he was one of the men who died in the mud-walled Roman fort some 250 miles north of Mombasa, the remains of which still stand. Mombasa was then the main port of East Africa and galleys waited there to be loaded with rice, sesame oil, ivory and wild animals for Italy. The fort may well have been put there as a way station for the animal collectors. If so, the local tribes would have long learned to avoid the place; otherwise they might at any time be pressed into service to haul the cages, or their fields stripped to feed the wild cargo. So the fort would have been isolated and the sentinels have no warning of an attack.

Perhaps at dawn, a Masai war party suddenly rushed the walls, giving their terrible yodeling cries as they hurled their spears and then drew their simis (long daggers) for the close work. The fort covers some five acres and the garrison was not strong enough to hold all the walls. Fulcinius would have fought to the end, side by side with his native troops and his big Molossian hounds which he used to drive animals aboard ship and to bring quarry to bay. Probably his trappers fought with their hunting spears, while the legionnaires used their swords and shields. At the end, they were overrun. Now only a few coins, some from the time of Nero, some of the time of Antoninus Pius, and one from the time of Trajan remain to show their fate. The victorious Masai left the coins on the ground but took the valuable weapons and armor from the dead men.

XIV

Up until the second century A.D., there still remained some sense of fair play in the games. A gladiator had a chance to leave the arena alive. He could even insist that the lanista put a price on him and if he could raise the sum he was free. An animal generally had a good chance to kill his human opponent, so the contest was often fairer than a modern bullfight. There was at least a pretense that the games were still contests— bloody, brutal and cruel but still retaining some idea of giving the contestants a sporting chance unless they were condemned criminals.

Gradually the games began to degenerate into spectacles of pointless massacre. People develop an immunity to scenes of cruelty and bloodshed and demand more and more ingenious methods to titivate their jaded interest. A favorite trick was to pit an armed man against an unarmed man. Naturally, the armed man always won. Then he was disarmed and another armed man sent out to kill him. This routine would go on all day.

Seneca, the famous philosopher, said of these exhibitions: "All previous games have been merciful, these are pure murder. The men have no defense, their bodies are open to every blow and every attack is bound to be successful. Most spectators

177

prefer this to the regular duels of skill. They would! Protection and training only postpone death, which is what the crowd have come to see."

Exhibitions like this began to take the place of the regular gladiatorial combats. Actually, a fight between two trained and evenly matched swordsmen is about as interesting as a chess tournament. It can go on for an hour or more and there's comparatively little action until the final thrust, each man conserving his strength and feeling out his opponent with light jabs and thrusts. The early Romans were all swordsmen themselves and could appreciate the fine points of combat, but the mob wanted something faster and bloodier, much as modern sports fans want to see plenty of action in a wrestling bout whereas honest wrestling is a slow business and a man may take twenty minutes to break a difficult hold.

Also, the shows had constantly to be "bigger and better than ever." Every emperor had to outdo his predecessors. Barnum and Bailey's went through a similar period. I remember a time when there were seven rings all going at once and no one had the slightest idea what was happening. By the end of the third century, there were a dozen amphitheaters in Rome, most of them in almost continuous operation. Some Of the best known were the Circus Maxentius on the Via Appia, the Circus Flaminus near the Circus Maximus, the Circus of Caligula-and-Nero where St. Peter's now stands, the Circus of Hadrian, the Circus Castrense (for the Praetorian Guard) and the Circus of Sallust. There was also, of course, the Flavian Amphitheater or Colosseum. Emperors stamped their coins with the heads of famous gladiators rather than their own images, and politicians had the number of games they gave engraved on their tombs.

What did these things cost? They finally got so expensive that the government and the aspiring politician had to share expenses to pay for a big spectacle. We only know what the government contributed toward these big games as we have only the governmental records. But it is almost impossible to translate the sums into, modern currency. Today, labor costs are the principal factor in any enterprise, while in Rome all labor was done by slaves. Then, too, trying to compute the sums in modern purchasing power is very difficult. For example, King Herod of Judea gave a series of games that cost him five hundred gold talents. Thomas H. Dyer in *Pompeii* (written in 1871) computes this sum as being equal roughly to 600,000. But Dyer wasn't thinking of the modern forty-cent dollar. Even computing Herod's five hundred talents as being worth $1,200,000, the actual purchasing power of the money at the time was far more. This doesn't take into consideration slave labor, gifts of gladiators and animals from subject kings, and contributions from private citizens who needed to stay in with the administration.

Simply to name some figures as a rough estimate, Titus' one hundred days of games which opened the Colosseum cost about eight million dollars, and the six days of Domitian's games described here cost about $36,000 a day. In 521 A.D., Justinian spent $910,000 on the games to celebrate his rise to power. Yet in 51 A.D. the total cost of all games for a year had been only $40,000. We know that the cost became a crushing one for any politician to carry. A magistrate named Milo exclaimed: "It's cost me three inheritances to stop the mouth of the people." But the shows continued. Although originally only the emperor or some great noble was permitted the honor of presenting the shows, by the second century any rich man could present them to advance himself socially—just as fifty years ago many a rich man in Great Britain discovered that public philanthropy was helpful in obtaining a title. Some games were put on by rich cobblers and wealthy tailors. Still, they continued to grow in magnificence.

After the triumph of the Emperor Aurelian over Zenobia, the warrior queen of Palmyra, in 272 A.D., Aurelian entered the arena in a chariot drawn by four stags, with Zenobia chained to the wheels by golden chains. He had a guard of twenty trained elephants, and two hundred other tamed animals walked in the procession. There was a "great host" of captives, each group led by a man with a placard around his neck giving the name of the tribe. The loot was carried in oxcarts heaped high with gold and jewels or on litters borne by slaves. In the games that followed, eight hundred pairs of gladiators fought as well as ten "Amazons", women fighters from some Middle Eastern tribe.

In 281 A.D., the Emperor Probus had "large trees torn up by the roots and fixed to beams in the arena. Sand was then spread over the beams so the whole circus resembled a forest. Into the arena were sent a thousand ostriches, a thousand stags, a thousand boars, one hundred lions, a hundred lionesses, a hundred leopards, three hundred bears and numerous other animals. These were all killed in a great hunt." (Vopiscus). Later, antelope were released and members of the crowd could amuse themselves trying to catch the animals. Sometimes naked girls were turned loose and any member of the crowd could keep anything he caught. Other emperors used silk imported from China for the awning instead of wool, had the nets employed to keep the animals off the podium woven of gold cords, plated the marble colonnades with gold and put mosaics of precious stones on the tier walls.

Sadism, instead of being incidental to the games, became the order of the day. Claudius used to order a wounded gladiator's helmet removed so he could watch the expression on the man's face while his throat was being cut. Girls were raped by men wearing the skins of wild beasts. Men were tied to rotting corpses and left to die. Children were suspended by their legs from the top of high poles for hyenas to pull down. So many victims were tied to stakes and then cut open that doctors used to attend the games in order to study anatomy.

Wholesale crucifixions in the arena became a major attraction, and the crowd would lay bets on who would be the first to die. As with every betting sport, a lot of time and trouble was devoted to fixing the business. By bribing an attendant, you could arrange to have a certain victim die almost immediately, last an hour, or live all day. If the spikes were driven in so as to cut an artery, the man would die in a few minutes. If driven so as to break the bones only, the man would live several hours. Occasionally, though, a victim would cross you up. He might deliberately pull at the spikes to make himself bleed to death or even beat his brains out against the upright. You could never be sure.

As far as being exhibitions of skill or courage, the games became a farce. Of course, there had always been scandals. Back in 60 A.D., a young charioteer had gone flying out of the chariot when his team made their usual jackrabbit start from the stalls. He was still given first prize. Still, the fact that he was the Emperor Nero might have had something to do with it. There was also the time when the Emperor Caligula had decided to auction off his victorious gladiators to a group of nobles. One man fell asleep and Caligula insisted on taking his nods for bids. When the man woke up, he found that he owned thirteen gladiators costing him nine million sesterces. However, generally people frowned on that sort of thing. Yet in 265 A.D., the Emperor Gallienus presented a wreath to a bullfighter who had missed the bull ten times. When the mob protested, the emperor explained via heralds, "It's not easy to miss as big an animal as a bull ten times running." Augustus had had to pass laws forbidding knights and senators from becoming gladiators, so eager were these men to show their valor in the arena. By the third century, no such laws were necessary. No one, patrician or plebeian, had any desire to climb into that arena.

For fifteen hundred years historians and, lately, psychologists have wondered why these games, which not only corrupted but bankrupted the greatest empire of all time, were such an obsession with the Roman mob. Orgies of death and suffering are forbidden today but we know they exert a strong fascination for most of us. Crowds gather around an automobile accident, go to bullfights, and block traffic if there's someone out on a high ledge threatening to commit suicide. Even the early Christians, who were themselves often sufferers in the arena, felt this intoxication with torture. St. Augustine tells of a young boy, Alypius, who was studying to be a monk. Some friends dragged him off to the arena against his will. Alypius sat with eyes closed and his fingers in his ears until an especially loud shout made him look. Two minutes later, he was out on his feet yelling, "Give him the sword! Cut his guts out!" He became an habitué of the games and gave up all thoughts of joining the church. St. Hilarion was such a devotee of the games that he could not stay away from them. He finally had to flee to the African desert where there were no circuses. Even so, in his dreams charioteers used to drive him like a horse and gladiators fight duels at the foot of his bed.

There is a definite connection between cruelty and sex, especially among weak, ineffectual people. Ovid remarked humorously, "Girls, if you can get a man to play with you while watching the games, he's yours." As the mob gradually lost all interest in finding work, serving in the legions or taking any civic responsibility, the games became increasingly more brutal and lewd. Finally they were simply excuses for sadistic debauches.

The more intelligent Romans were perfectly conscious of this deadly trend but they were helpless to prevent it. Augustus tried to limit the games to two a year. He found it impossible. Marcus Aurelius, who defined the games as an "expensive bore," passed a law that the gladiators had to fight with blunted weapons. The popular opposition was such that he not only had to rescind the order but even ended by increasing the number of games from 87 to 230 a year. His annual bill for gladiators alone was $2,500,000. Vespasian, who was famous for being a tightwad and swore that he was going to put an end to this game nonsense, finished by building the Colosseum.

Curiously, the Roman philosophers were almost unanimous in their endorsement of the games. Cicero said, "It does the people good to see that even slaves can fight bravely. If a mere slave can show such courage, what then can a Roman do? Besides, the games harden a warrior people to sights of carnage and prepares them for battle." Tacitus couldn't understand why Tiberius didn't like the fights and quotes the emperor's habit of turning away from scenes of slaughter as a sign of weakness in his character. Pliny speaks of the games approvingly and so do many other serious thinkers.

Almost the only Roman philosopher who came out openly against the games was Seneca, who lived at the time of Nero. He records a conversation he had with a spectator at a show.

"But," my neighbor says to me, "that man whom you pity was a highway robber."

"Very well, then hang him, but why nail him to a cross and set wild beasts on him?"

"But he killed a man."

"Let him be condemned to death in his turn. He deserves it. But you, what have you done that you should be condemned to watch such a spectacle?"

Seneca was cordially disliked and finally committed suicide by order of Nero.

Originally only a few criminals of the worst type were killed in the arena but when it became obvious that the mob regarded these killings as the main attraction, holocausts of victims were arranged. Finding enough prisoners for these spectacles became increasingly difficult. Probably the persecution of the Christians eventually became only another way of getting fresh fodder for the arena.

The first of the Christian persecutions were under Nero. According to Roman historians, Nero dreamed of turning Rome from a rabbit warren of twisting streets and wooden slums into a city of marble. He also wanted to clear away a large section in the center of the city where he could build a palace worthy of him—"The Golden House." Later, the Colosseum was built on the site of the Golden House as an apology to the people. Nero's agents fired the city but popular resentment forced the emperor to find a scapegoat. He settled on the despised and suspected sect called Christians.

Tacitus tells us: "Nero had all admitted Christians seized. These informed on others who were also arrested, not so much for setting fire to the city as for their hatred of mankind. Everything was done to make their deaths humiliating. They were dressed in animal skins and torn to pieces by dogs, crucified, or covered with pitch and used as torches to light the arena after dark. Although as Christians they deserved punishment, still people felt that they were being punished to satisfy the emperor's love of cruelty and not for the good of the nation."

Suetonius supplies some other details. Nero used to dress himself up as a lion or a leopard and attack the private parts of men and women tied to stakes in the arena. Afterwards, one of his freemen named Doryphorus would enter the arena dressed as a venador and pretend to kill the emperor. It was probably exhibitions like this that caused St. John to speak of the arena as the "mother of fornication . . . the church of sacred sanguinary." Nero also spent large sums trying to locate a legendary Egyptian ogre who was supposed to kill and eat people. Nero wanted to exhibit him in the arena. The ogre never turned up.

Some of the most terrible persecutions of the Christians took place under Marcus Aurelius in 166 A.D. Marcus Aurelius was one of the most enlightened emperors Rome ever had, but he didn't like Christians. As pacifists, Christians refused to serve in the legions at a critical period when the barbarian hordes were breaching the defenses on all sides, they denounced wealth which made the Romans regard them as dangerous radicals, and they refused to sacrifice to the emperor's genius— roughly equivalent today to refusing to salute the flag or repeat the oath of allegiance. Scratched on a wall in Rome there is a crude drawing showing a donkey nailed to a cross with the legend below: "All Christians are donkeys." Marcus Aurelius decided to stamp out this vicious cult and went about it systematically.

Records by the early church fathers tell us that Christians in the arena had red-hot plates of iron strapped to their bodies, their flesh was torn from their bones with hot pincers, they were chained in iron seats over fires, and roasted on spits. Eusebius tells of the death of Blandina; one of these martyrs. She was first forced to watch the death of her friends in the arena. When that didn't break her resolve, she was made to run the gantlet between two lines of men armed with whips and iron bars. She was then hung from a pole as bait for starved hyenas and wolves. Half-dead, she was cut down and forced to watch her little brother flogged, burned over a fire and finally flung to wild beasts—constantly told that if she would recant, the child's life would be spared. As Blandina still stood firm, she was finally put in a net and swung from the scaffolding of the arena for wild bulls to gore.

We have an eye witness account of these martyrdoms left us by two brothers, Felix and Verus Macarius. The events described took place on October 11, 290 A.D. under the Emperor Maximus.

"The stadium was crowded; Maximus also attended. A number of wild beasts being let loose, many criminals were devoured. We Christians in the stands kept ourselves concealed and were awaiting with great fear to see the martyrs brought forth. The martyrs were Tharacus, Probus, and Andronicus. They were carried by other condemned people, having been tortured so they could not walk. They looked so pitiful that we wept, hiding our faces so the crowd would not notice. They were tossed like refuse on the sand. Many people murmured and Maximus shouted to the soldiers. 'Note those people. They'll be down with those Christians if they're so fond of them.'

"The wild beasts were let loose, especially a very frightful bear; then a lioness. Both roared fearfully at each other but did not attack the martyrs, much less devour them. The Master of the Games became enraged and commanded the spear-men to kill them. The bear was pierced through but the lioness made her escape through a door left open by some of the bestiarii who ran away in terror. Then Maximus commanded the Master of the Games to let the gladiators kill the Christians and afterwards fight to the death among themselves. When this tragedy was over, Maximus before he left the podium ordered ten soldiers to mutilate both the martyrs and the gladiators so the Christians couldn't tell them apart."

It was usual for Christians to bribe the arena slaves for the bodies of the martyrs so that they could be given decent burial.

How many Christians were martyred we have no idea. Tacitus only says that Nero "killed a great multitude of Christians." However, later we have a few statistics. During the persecutions under Maximus, nineteen hundred Christians were martyred in Sicily alone. Diocletian killed seventeen thousand in one month. Eusebius says that during one of the persecutions, ten thousand men (not counting women and children) were killed in Egypt. The executioners blunted their swords and had to work in relays. Of course, compared to Hitler, who killed 2,500,000 people in concentration camps within a few years, this is pretty small potatoes, but the Romans did their best.

Very few of the Christians recanted, although an altar with a fire burning on it was generally kept in the arena for their convenience. All a prisoner had to do was scatter a pinch of incense on the flame and he was given a Certificate of Sacrifice and turned free. It was also carefully explained to him that he was not worshiping the emperor; merely acknowledging the divine character of the emperor as head of the Roman state. Still, almost no Christians availed themselves of the chance to escape. Naturally, there were a few exceptions. Polycarp tells of one man in a provincial amphitheater who held out until actually in the arena. Then he collapsed and begged to be allowed to sacrifice. The editor refused and demanded that the animals be released. The only animal was a lion who had been starved to make him savage. But the bestiarius had overdone it and when the lion was released, the poor brute just lay down and died. The martyr had to be burned at the stake.

By the end of the fourth century, the games had fallen into the hands of promoters and the spirit of competition had virtually disappeared. The charioteers had organized a powerful union and now demanded that a man had to be allowed a certain number of wins. A charioteer might race for the Blues in one race and for the Greens in the next. He did not know what horses he would have before he climbed into the chariot—a far cry from Diocles and his perfectly trained teams. The gladiator was finished as a highly trained professional. Obtaining sufficient wild animals for the games had become almost impossible: Europe, north Africa and Asia Minor had been swept bare. The Romans were even running out of Christians, Jews and criminals for the spectacles.

A series of letters left by a senator named Quintus Aurelius Symmachus shows what a problem giving a series of games had become. Symmachus wanted to put on a week's games in honor of his son who had just been made an officer in the swagger Praetorian Guard and would run for praetor in 401 A.D. Symmachus started preparing for the games two years ahead of time.

Symmachus, in addition to being a senator, was a very wealthy man. He owned three palaces and had held nearly every high office in the state. Being a devout man. Symmachus was greatly shocked at the growth of this new cult called Christianity, and he determined to put on some real old-fashioned games to impress the people with scenes of skill and courage in order to disgust them with the namby-pamby doctrines of the new religion. The Master of the Games tried to talk the senator out of putting on anything but the usual run of stuff then current, but Symmachus insisted that he wanted the real thing.

Poor Symmachus ran into nothing but headaches. To get really well-trained chariot horses, Symmachus had to import them from Spain. The nags used in Rome by then were only good enough to go around the track in a fixed race and stage a few smash-ups for the crowd. Eleven out of the sixteen horses Symmachus imported died before they reached the arena from bad handling on the voyage. The four left were so much better than the ordinary chariot horses that the race would have been a walk-away so the team had to be broken up. As a result, their charioteer quit.

Four other charioteers were collected and more horses imported. Then it was discovered that the best charioteer was a Christian. As the whole point of the show was to prove that the weak Christians couldn't compete with the manly adherents of the old Roman religion, he had to be fired. But as he was a member of the union; the union called a strike. In a rage, Symmachus threatened to stage a race using dogs instead of horses because, as he said, the regular chariot horses were nothing but dogs anyhow. This caused a riot in which the Praetorian Guard had to be called out.

Meanwhile, Symmachus was trying hard to get wild animals for the games. He wrote to animal collectors, to friends in distant provinces, to officials, pointing out that they should cooperate in this great crusade to put on some really good shows to restore national morale. He spent months trying to unscramble the red tape. As professional collectors were now scarce, he had to hire his own men. This meant that he had to get them trapping licenses, as lions and elephants could only be trapped by special permission of the emperor. He had to get special permission to give the shows in the Colosseum. The customs officials charged him an import tax on the animals although, as Symmachus explained in letter after letter, this tax was meant only to apply to professional dealers who retailed their animals after arrival.

In spite of all this trouble, Symmachus couldn't get any lions, tigers, elephants or even antelope (he wanted topi and impala especially). All that arrived were some "weak and starving bear cubs" and a few crocodiles. The crocs hadn't eaten for fifty days and most of them had to be killed before the shows. Apparently the only animals that arrived in fit condition were some Irish wolfhounds.

Symmachus had even more trouble getting gladiators. He managed to purchase twenty-nine Saxon prisoners, supposed to be terrific fighters, but the prisoners never got out of gladiatorial school. They strangled each other until there was only one man left—and he beat his brains out against the wall.

What sort of games Symmachus finally did put on, I don't know. We only have his correspondence trying to get the acts lined up. We do know that the seven days' games cost him $456,750, and I'll bet his son never did get elected praetor.

By the beginning of the fifth century, Rome found herself fighting for her life against the barbarian hordes along her frontiers. With the tremendous cost of the continual wars, it became increasingly difficult to pay for the games. Yet they continued, always catering more and more to the mob. The emperors abandoned the royal box as being undemocratic and sat with the crowd. The patricians made a great point of eating the food thrown to the mob instead of leaving the amphitheaters for lunch or having slaves serve their own repast.

The chariot races were a joke. People threw wine jars in front of the horses' feet and women encouraged their children to dart under the opposing teams hoping to make their team win. If the child was trampled, the indignant parents sued the racing stables for reckless driving. The crowd still continued to call themselves Blues, Greens, and so on, even though they no longer knew anything about the horses or the men. A somewhat similar trend has occurred in modern big league baseball. Once every man on a team was a local boy; the crowds knew each player individually and turned out to root for friends. Today, the teams are recruited from men all over the country and are sold as commodities without any regard for community feelings. Pliny's remark about the chariot factions would apply today: "The people know only the color." Yet with no political parties and no feeling of belonging to any specific group, the people centered all their devotion on being a White or a Gold. People who were born Reds swore eternal enmity toward all other factions, supported the Reds under all circumstances, and considered a Green victory a national disaster.

With the economic and military position of the empire too hopelessly complicated for the crowd to comprehend, they turned more and more toward the only thing that they could understand—the arena. The name of a great general or a brilliant statesman meant no more to the Roman mob than the name of a great scientist does to us today. But the average Roman could tell you every detail of the last games, just as today the average man can tell you all about a movie star's marriages but has only the foggiest idea what NATO is doing or what steps are being taken to fight inflation.

For an ambitious man to get anywhere in public life, he had to establish a tie-in with the games. The Emperor Vitellius had been a groom for the Blues. As a result, he was made governor of Germany by a politician who was a Blue. After Vitellius became emperor, he had anyone killed who booed the Blues. The Emperor Commodus went to gladiator's school and used to fight in the arena to win popular support. The Emperor Macrinus had been a professional gladiator. Even finding victims enough to be killed in the arena became a serious drain on the empire. "We are sacrificing the living to feed the dead," protested Caracalla, referring to the fact that the games were supposedly given to appease the souls of the departed. Yet the games kept on. Without them, the mob could not be controlled, and by now the entire national economy was tied up with the great spectacles. To have stopped them would have caused as serious a crisis as if our government suddenly abandoned dams, farm relief, and military spending.

Yet the end could not be postponed forever. Rome began to be overrun by foreigners. Thousands of Gauls, Germans, and

Parthians were living in the city, brought there to bolster the weakening empire. These "barbarians" had no interest in the games which, after all, required a rather special taste to appreciate. A Parthian prince left the circus in disgust, remarking, "It's no fun seeing people killed who haven't a chance." The crowd yelled, "Burr-head! Why doncha go back to Parthia where ya belong?" but the savages gradually obtained the balance of power. After all, the emperors depended on these foreign auxiliaries for support and placating the Roman mob became less and less important.

The Christian church was growing in power and did everything possible to stop the games. In 325 A.D., Constantine tried to put an end to the games but they still continued. Then in 365 A.D., Valentinian forbade sacrificing victims to wild beasts. He was able to make his edict stick, and that took all the fun out of the spectacles. In 399 A.D. the gladiatorial schools had to close for want of pupils.

Then in 404 A.D., a monk named Telemachus leaped into the arena and appealed to the people to stop the fights. Telemachus was promptly stoned to death by the angry mob but his death ended the spectacles. The Emperor Honorius was so furious at Telemachus' lynching that he closed the arenas. They were never reopened. The last chariot race was held after the fall of Rome by Tolila, a Goth, in 549 A.D. He was merely curious to see what the business looked like.

Yet so deeply had the games entered into the national consciousness that people still considered themselves as supporting the Red, White, Green or Blue faction—although many of these people had no idea what the colors meant. In 532 A.D., riots broke out between the Blues and the Greens that threatened to wreck what remained of the empire. The Emperor Justinian had to call out troops to restore peace, and in the fighting over thirty thousand people were killed.

The only remaining relics of these titanic spectacles are some crude pictures scratched on the walls of gladiator barracks, a few cracked tombstones, references in the literature of the times and, here and there, the ruins of the amphitheaters. The games followed the legionnaires as chewing gum follows American GIs, and wherever the legions were stationed there was sure to be a circus. Roman governors built stadiums as soon as they arrived in their province, confident that this was the only way to keep the population contended. Many of their letters express amazement that the Greeks, Gauls and Britons seemed more interested in having enough to eat than in watching the games.

Establishing these amphitheaters was a difficult job. The Greeks fought them to the last (Plutarch describes the games as "bloody and brutal") but in other countries the games slowly gained a following, although they never enjoyed anything like the popularity they had in Rome, Egypt held out against them for a long time but at last had to yield—in every nation there is always a certain proportion of people who enjoy such sights. So all over the Roman world great amphitheaters appeared, hardly less magnificent than the ones in Rome itself: at Capus, Pompeii, Pozzuoli and Verona in Italy; at Arles and Nimes in France; at Seville in Spain; at Antioch in Palestine; at Alexandria in Egypt; at Silchester in Britain; at El Djem in Tunisia.

Many of these amphitheaters still remain. You can sit in the "maeniana" (stands) with a cold chicken and a bottle of wine and speculate out of which door the animals were released, where the inner barrier ran, and how they got the lions out of the "cavea" (interior) into the arena. As your guess is probably as good as anyone's, it's an interesting way to spend an afternoon.

The largest amphitheater remaining is, of course, the Colosseum. Although the prodigious structure has been used as a quarry for a thousand years and a large part of Medieval

Rome was built with stone taken from it, much still remains. Byron wrote:

A ruin! Yet what ruin! from its mass
Walls, palaces, half-cities, have been rear'd;
Yet oft the enormous skeleton ye pass,
And marvel where the spoil could have appear'd.

You can crawl through the "enormous skeleton" with a copy of J. H. Middleton's *The Remains of Ancient Rome* and go nuts trying to find all the places he mentioned. You can see the huge travertine blocks used in the construction, some seven feet long, and held together with iron clamps as mere mortar couldn't carry the fantastic strain put on them. In the Middle Ages when iron was desperately needed, people dug thousands of these clamps out of the stone, a murderously laborious job. Although as late as 1756, a French archeologist computed that there was still 17,000,000 francs (roughly about $80,000) worth of marble remaining in the Colosseum, almost all of it is now gone. However, you can still see many of the carved marble curale chairs used by the patricians on the podium. They're in Italian churches being used as episcopal thrones.

Next to the Colosseum, the largest of the remaining amphitheaters is in Verona, Italy. It is 502 feet long by 401 feet wide and 98 feet high. It held about thirty thousand people and is still used for the mild Italian bullfights. The next largest remaining circus is in Nimes, France. It measures 435 by 345 feet and held about twenty thousand people. It is two stories high with 124 entrances. The Pompeian amphitheater is comparatively small but interesting because it is so well-preserved and the gladiator barracks are nearby.

In the Middle Ages these amphitheaters were regarded

with superstitious awe. People living in Pola, Italy, thought the amphitheater there must have been built by supernatural beings as no mortal man could accomplish such a task. They claimed that the stadium was a fairy palace, built in a single night. They explained the fact that the building had no roof by saying that a cock was awakened by the hammering and crew: the fairies thought it was daybreak and left without finishing the job.

Many of the amphitheaters were used as fortresses during the Middle Ages. Some of them were used as barns and crops were planted in the arenas. The farmers were astonished at how well the crops grew, not knowing that the soil was well fertilized.

The *ludi,* as the Romans called the games, were not, of course, games in our modern sense. Nor were they merely spectacles or shows as we understand the terms. They were a vital and integral part of Roman life and psychology. The closest modern parallel would be the Spanish bullfight which to a Latin is an emotional experience rather than a sport or an exhibition of skill. For over five hundred years the *ludi* continued in one form or other. Hundreds of generations of Romans were born, grew up and died under their influence. At last, they came completely to dominate the life of the average inhabitant of Rome. His one interest—almost his one cause of living—was to attend the *ludi.*

The growth, character, and final degeneration of the *ludi* closely paralleled the growth, character and degeneration of the Roman Empire. In the old, simple days of the republic, the games were simply athletic contests. As Rome became a conquering power, the games became bloody, ruthless and fierce, although still retaining a conception of fair play and sportsmanship. This was the era when Augustus had to pass laws forbidding patricians from jumping into the arena and fighting it out with professional gladiators, and a young noble would challenge a victorious German prisoner to a fight to the death. When Rome finished her conquests and became merely a despotic power, the games became pointlessly cruel. Toward the end they were nothing but sadistic displays. Shortly after this period, the empire collapsed.

Any modern promoter who cared to put on a series of shows duplicating the Roman games would easily be able to fill the house. Mickey Spillane could be Master of the Games. Bullfights, cockfights, dogfights, and the Indianapolis Speedway (our closest approach to the chariot races) are all popular. I even find it hard to believe that all boxing fans are primarily interested in the fine points of the sport rather than in seeing two men half kill each other. If they knew that one man really would be killed, they'd enjoy it all the more. The most popular programs on TV are the Westerns showing men shooting each other. The next most popular are the gangster films. Of course, the men don't actually kill each other—if they did you couldn't get people away from their sets.

The Roman games were probably the biggest argument against "spectator sports" that can be advanced. As long as the Romans were themselves a nation of fighting men, there might have been some truth to the beliefs of Cato and Pliny that the games encouraged manly virtues. But there is a big difference between tough fighting men, appreciatively watching a struggle between equally matched opponents, and a depraved crowd gloating over scenes of meaningless cruelty.

The same tendency can be seen today in rough sports. The spectator who hollers, "Murder the burns! Knock his teeth out! Kill him!" is usually a meek little guy in a rear seat who has just got a bawling out from his boss and had to sneak out of the house when his wife wasn't home. He wants to see somebody else getting hurt . . . he doesn't care who.

AUTHOR'S NOTE

So many sources were used in preparing this volume that it would be impossible to name them all. In many cases, only a single reference was taken from a book. However, some of the main works dealing with the games are listed in the Bibliography. Some of the sequences, especially in the description of the shows at the time of Carpophorus, are a compendium of many sources. In describing how Carpophorus trained the animals that had relations with women, I used Apuleius and also the technique employed by a Mexican gentleman I met in Tia Juana who was making 16mm stag films on the subject.

The description of the ventores' battle with lions and tigers is a combination of original sources, J.A. Hunter's account of Masai warriors spearing lions, and comments from Mel Koontz and Marbel Stark, both of whom are professional lion tamers. The crocodile wrestling is described by Strabo, but I added material told me by a Seminole Indian who wrestled alligators in Florida. The gladiatorial combats are all taken from contemporary accounts or from graffiti (wall drawings) in Pompeii. The bullfights are from graffiti of the fights, contemporary descriptions, the murals in Cnossus, incidents I've observed in Spanish bullfights, and suggestions made by Pete Patterson, who is a rodeo clown.

The battle between the Essedarii and the Greek Hoplites is a combination of Tacitus' descriptions of British war chariots, Hogarth's description of the Hoplite phalanx in *Philip and Alexander of Macedon,* extracts from Mason's *Roping,* and the manner in which British square was handled in the early nineteenth century. The elephant fights come from contemporary sources and Capt. Fitz-Bernard, who saw war elephants in India.

The description of Chilo's tavern is taken from Amedeo Maiuri's *Pompeii* and my own notes on a wine shop there. The conversation between the men is nearly all from Petronius' *Satyricon.* Although my account of Carpophorus' death is completely fictitious, polar bears were seen in the arena, possibly as early as Nero's reign. The Romans did believe that the narwhal's horn was that of a unicorn. The narwhal, being a mammal like a whale or dolphin, can produce ivory.

BIBLIOGRAPHY

Darstellungen aus der Sittengeschihte Roms, L. Friedlander
Animals for Show and Pleasure in Ancient Rome, George Jennison
The Spectacles, Martial
The Remains of Ancient Rome, J. H. Middleton
Trebaid, Statius
Historia Ecclesiastica, Eusebius
Martyr's Mirror, Thielem von Bracht
Acts of the Martyrs, P. I. Twisck
Pompeii, Thomas H. Dyer
Philip and Alexander of Macedon, David G. Hogarth
Les Gladiateurs dans l'orient Grec, Louis Robert
Roping, Bernard Mason
Fighting Sports, Capt. L. Fitz-Barnard
The Satyricon, Petronius
The Memoirs of Diocles
And the writings of Tacitus, Suetonius, Apuleius

ABOUT THE AUTHOR

Daniel P. Mannix was an award-winning American author and journalist, as well as a magician and filmmaker. Mannix's magazine articles about his experiences in the carnival, where he performed under the stage name "The Great Zadma," became popular in the mid-1940s and were compiled with the assistance of his wife in the book *Step Right Up!* His dozens of books and extensive essays range in subject from children's animal stories, environmental issues, and hunting accounts to historical examinations of the Hellfire Club, the Atlantic slave trade, and the Roman gladiatorial games. Mannix was particularly interested in the Wizard of Oz canon and composed a biography of L. Frank Baum for *American Heritage* magazine in the 1960s.

INTEGRATED MEDIA